Willem van der Eyken
and Barry Turner

Adventures in Education

Allen Lane The Penguin Press

First published in 1969

Allen Lane The Penguin Press,
Vigo Street, London W1

SBN 7139 0094 6

Printed by Hazell Watson & Viney Ltd,
Aylesbury, Bucks

Contents

List of Plates

Introduction

Educational historians are in love with legislation. When they try to trace the path of progress, they invariably turn to Hansard and the lofty sentiments of Royal Commissions. Their dates pay respect to the passing of complex Acts that put change on to the Statute Book. But in doing so they confuse the processes by which change in education comes about. Their work not only implies, wrongly, that Parliament is an instigator rather than a recorder of change, but that improvements in standards of living, brought about through economic growth, are synonymous with advances in educational thought and practice.

Yet a hard look inside classrooms and lecture halls shows this is far from the case. In many ways, and despite the vastly different physical conditions that exist today, the educational 'industry' resists change. Corporal punishment, that black dwarf of schooldays, is still with us. Selection remains a stubborn element of our system. At fifteen, half our children still rush out of school, glad to escape what they regard as an irrelevance. In our universities, teaching methods are fundamentally much the same as they were in the founding days of Salerno, Bologna and Paris. We still regard children under five as ineducable. Our method of producing teachers is probably the most wasteful any society has ever devised. Many schools cling to Latin and Greek in preference to science and economics. But logic, Plato's prime subject, is nowhere to be found. We still incarcerate children in vast gloomy buildings and isolate them both from their parents and relatives as well as the world for

7

which they are supposed to be being prepared. It is a depressing record.

Yet there is a credit side. Among the vast army of teachers, administrators and inspectors who operate this system, there have always been a number who, often in the teeth of conservative resistance, have pressed new ideas to the attention of their colleagues. By their enthusiasm, skill and devotion – or, if you prefer, stubbornness – they have created new attitudes, new yardsticks. The twentieth century, which has seen the monolithic structure of British education secularized and decentralized, has been a rich time for these pioneers. It has not sought them, but neither has it turned them away. It is they who have provided the Research and Development element of the 'industry'.

But because of the peculiar nature of education, which does not consciously seek to improve itself but absorbs improvements like a sponge, their efforts have met with mixed success. Their innovations have had to fight against a rigid examination framework and the natural forces of mediocrity and inertia. Sometimes the very processes of history have been against them.

These opposing forces have made the innovators a particularly hardy band; some might say eccentric. Very often they have come from outside the system itself, believing that education is too important a subject to be left to the educators. Sometimes their particular contributions, so relevant in their own day, have faded away with time. Ideas must not merely be new; they must have stamina. Their backers need courage and energy. They have to call upon a good deal of ingenuity. And if their ideas are to survive and influence the course of events, they need the luck of good timing.

The 'history' of education is rich with such people, and their contributions have often been neglected, even ignored. In an attempt to draw attention to their efforts, and to preserve the detail of their endeavours before the participants leave the stage, we have collated some of their stories here. This book is, in a sense, an exercise in the 'archaeology of education', digging up half-submerged incidents, voices already retired from active life, torn newspapers, faded broadsheets, dusty trunks in attics. Our choice was never intended to be comprehensive : we have deliberately avoided some legendary, and well-chronicled, figures. We do not even claim that the innovators of whom we write were successful; not all were. Or that they were more important, or less, than others we might have chosen. We offer them, rather, as representatives of a species whose creativity and enterprise has enriched the thinking and practice of education today.

The Malting House School, the subject of the first adventure, is a classic case. One of its founders, Susan Isaacs, is a household name to thousands of student teachers, and the influence of the school itself is apparent, through those teachers, in every good primary school in the land. Yet what is not known about this innovation is how great a part was played by a man, Geoffrey Pyke, who had nothing whatever to do with the educational Establishment, the Rolls to Susan Isaacs' Royce. The story of their joint experiment is more than a tragic human episode; it displays all the characteristics of a pioneering effort in education : vision, enterprise, single-minded effort, strong personalities, chance, opportunism. It began as an attempt by a father to provide a new education for his only son. It apparently foundered after five short years, and yet its influence permeated the entire education system. One of the reasons for this was Pyke's extraordinary network of connexions at Cambridge, and Susan Isaacs' subsequent work at the Institute of Education at London University.

The second story, of the little known Burston Rebellion, also had more than its fair share of public attention, and yet here we deal with a failure, if we are to judge purely on the question of subsequent influence. But what a glorious failure! For here were born the seeds of a great revolution, whose vision was an education system by the people for the people, at a time when the schools were in the hands of an autocracy. The story of the Higdons, and their local feud, is a small stone in the crazy paving of modern educational reform. The First World War cut across its influence like a knife, shearing it off from modern

Introduction

developments, and placing it firmly in its post-Victorian setting. When the war ended, the world was permanently changed, and events moved in another direction, towards other battles.

Burston was an interesting near miss. The rise of arts and crafts, on the other hand, was a direct hit. In the area of educational development, this adventure has the true evolutionary quality so inherent in much of reform, but so difficult to trace in any specific instance. Here, in the rise of artwork in the classroom, and in the recognition of the child as artist, there was no sudden revelation, no one single experiment which proved the case conclusively. It was a long, heavy haul, by a large number of teachers working often in isolation from one another, towards a goal which today is recognized and admired as one of the most creative flowerings of our primary schools. It has, too, another characteristic : the inter-relationship of teachers and the Inspectorate. This last group, so influential an element in British education, has been much ignored, even by specialists. In the opportunity of looking at the work of one H.M.I., Robin Tanner – admittedly a larger-than-life example of the breed – we seized a chance to study this influence, and the way that it acted as a spur to innovation.

One of the reasons why both the Malting House School and the rise of arts and crafts proved successful in influencing the course of education was that they were 'mainstream' experiments, involving those, like Susan Isaacs, Marion Richardson and Tanner, who could maintain a direct conversation with the daily practice in the schools, and shape the views of those in authority. The Forest School experiment, while it contained the seeds of genuine revolution in educational thinking, had no such contact. It was a 'one-off' isolated venture, drawing its strength from two remarkable men, but without that built-in stamina that pushed the ideas beyond a small, select circle of devotees. It suffered, as did Burston, through the imminence of a world war, but it has left a legacy in the Forest School camps, which continue to this day. Its relative obscurity demands a longer discussion of innovation in education than can be afforded here. Many of the ideas that it put forward are contained in the recent Newsom and Plowden reports, and its implied criticism of the state education service has as much relevance today as it did in the twenties. Yet it failed. That is its interest. Some of the school buildings in the New Forest still stand, gaunt reminders that ideas, and vigour, and dedication are not enough if education is to change. More ingredients are needed.

What those ingredients are is not clear, but the final adventure in this book, the story of Henry Morris, provides some clues. Here, again, is a case of the innovator working within the system he seeks to change, with, in his case, the power to change it at least at the local level. Most critics would accept that Morris's innovations have helped to shape modern education as the Forest School has not, and yet, with the passing of time, it is possible to see that Morris, too, lacked one essential feature that prevented him from accomplishing a true revolution in learning. It was timing. Events overtook him. One of the most creative polymaths modern education has thrown up, Morris brought to his subject wide reading, intense vision, and a degree of ruthlessness and dedication which make his reign in Cambridge as Chief Education Officer one of the most fertile of any administrator. Moreover, he demonstrated that it was not only teachers, nor even inspectors, who could bring about radical change. All of life can be an adventure, if we are disposed to make it so.

*

It is one of the features of this book that none of the five stories it contains has been related before. In presenting them, we are indebted to a countless number of people who helped us with our search, who dug through their files and their reminiscences for us, who checked other people's memories, and who allowed us to trespass upon their hospitality, in some cases many times, in order to verify facts and find new material.

The story of The Malting House School was written by Willem van der Eyken, and built up from interviews with the late Margaret Pyke, widow of Geoffrey Pyke; with the late Nathan

Introduction

Isaacs, husband of Dr Susan Isaacs, and on a study of the papers of Geoffrey Pyke, in the possession of his son, Dr David Pyke. It is also based on interviews and correspondence with nearly a dozen of the school's former pupils and three of its former teachers, and on records of legal proceedings brought against Pyke in 1929 and 1930. (It may be of interest that as a result of this study, these papers, placed with the Registry Office, London, are to be preserved for a period longer than would otherwise have been the case.)

The writing of the Burston Rebellion, by Barry Turner, was based on a pamphlet published by the Labour Press; on papers in the possession of local residents of the village; on the records of the Agricultural Workers' Union; on the files of the National Union of Teachers; and on extracts from the *Eastern Daily Press* newspaper.

The stories of Marion Richardson and Robin Tanner, by Willem van der Eyken, were built up almost entirely from interviews with those involved. Chief among these were Robin Tanner, Christian Schiller, Edith Moorhouse, Geoffrey Elsmore, James Fairbairn, Christine Smale, John Blackie, Ruth Wertheimer, David Evans, Tom John and George Baines – all either inspectors or teachers who have played a major role in the rise of arts and crafts in the primary school. The stories also draw on Marion Richardson's own book, *Art and the Child*, published in 1948 by the University of London Press, and on notes and records of teachers' meetings and conferences held at Leeds, Oxford, London and Dartington. A unique collection of children's art from 1922 onwards, in the possession of Robin Tanner, was also used.

The story of Ernest Westlake and the Forest School, by Willem van der Eyken, was compiled from sources that included the Centenary Tribute presented by his son, Dr Aubrey Westlake, to the Conference of Educational Associations in London in 1956; Westlake's own writings, included in the Woodcraft Way series published by the British Order of Woodcraft Chivalry between 1919 and 1933; and the private papers of the school, some of them kept in a suitcase in a solicitor's office in

Wincanton. It was also based on the personal reminiscences of many people, including Dorothy Glaister, Rachel Rutter, Tom Rutter and Ronald Brand. Robert Mackenzie, a teacher at the school, generously allowed us to consult his own writings, as yet unpublished, about the school.

The story of Henry Morris and the Cambridge village colleges, by Barry Turner, is based on Morris's papers – including his letters, speeches and broadcasts – collected by his secretary, Miss Bimrose, and held by the Henry Morris Memorial Trust, which kindly allowed us access to them. It was amplified by interviews with many people who worked with Morris or had dealings with him, and in particular George Edwards, Chief Education Officer for Cambridgeshire and the Isle of Ely, who was Morris's deputy for eleven years, and Jack Pritchard, one of Morris's life-long friends.

We are in debt to all these people, and many more. In particular, we would like to thank David Duguid, who read the manuscript and gave us critical but constructive advice, and those who loaned us photographs and prints, of inestimable value to themselves, readily and without reservation. Among these are Ivan J. Underwood for the picture of Burston Strike School, and the chief librarian of Norwich Public Library for pictures of the Burston Rebellion; Dr David Pyke for the stills taken from the Mary Field production on the Malting House School; Mr Robin Tanner for the photographs of Ivy Lane School and the examples of children's art from his personal collection; Mrs Dorothy Glaister for the photographs of Forest School; the *Architectural Review* for the picture of Impington Village College and Mr Jack Pritchard for the portrait of Henry Morris.

None of these people is responsible in any way for the final interpretations we have placed upon their documents, their memories and their deeds.

The Malting House School : 1924-9

When I first came to the school I tried to decide what was the most striking difference between this school and any other I have known. I came to the conclusion that it is the happiness of the children.
Dr Evelyn Lawrence, 1927

In the *New Statesman* of 1 March 1924, amongst articles on Ramsay Macdonald's new Labour government, the weakness of Poincaré's regime, the suppression of truth in Mussolini's Italy, and the slowness of London buses, there appeared the following half-page advertisement :

Wanted. An Educated Young Woman, 18-27, to conduct the education of a small group of children, aged $2\frac{1}{2}$-7, as a piece of scientific work and research.

A Liberal Salary – liberal as compared with either research work or teaching – will be paid to a suitable applicant who will live out, have fixed hours and opportunities for a pleasant independent existence. An assistant will be provided when the work increases.

The advertisers wish to get in touch with someone possessing certain personal qualifications for the work, and a scientific attitude of mind towards it. Previous educational experience is by no means required, but training in any one of the natural sciences is a distinct advantage.

The applicant chosen would require to undergo a course of preliminary training, 6-8 months, in London. In part, at any rate, the expense of this being paid by the advertisers. The advertisers would also welcome correspondence from others with similar needs.

The same advertisement, enlarged to a full page, appeared again two weeks later in the same journal, and on 22 March a further full page suggested that the young woman, who should have an honours degree, would not be barred if she had had no previous educational experience :

But the advertisers hope to get in touch with a university graduate or someone of equivalent intellectual standing – who has hitherto considered themselves too good for teaching and who has probably already engaged in another occupation.

These unusual, compelling advertisements were written and paid for by a man called Geoffrey Nathaniel Pyke, who was later to be described in *The Times* as 'one of the most original if unrecognized figures of the present century'. Pyke, by history and make-up, was a man apart. His father, a Jewish lawyer, died when he was still a young boy. His mother, wilful, proud, left with four children to bring up by herself, insisted on sending him to Wellington, where he was teased and bullied unmercifully, and then later to Pembroke College, Cambridge, to read Law. He never completed his studies, leaving Cambridge in his second year, but the fact that he did not take a degree and was therefore not eligible for a university post always remained a thorn in his side.

Geoffrey Pyke rejected his mother. He seldom mentioned her in conversation, and later in life turned away from her, never to see her again. This rejection, coupled with the absence of a father, isolated him. His Jewish origins, his tall, gangling figure, his restless curiosity, all contributed to make him different from his companions. Above all, his unorthodoxy or, as a friend once described it, his 'arch simplicity', in thought, in manner and in dress – he once brought his fiancée to dine with some friends, wearing hiking boots – cut him off from others. 'I've learnt to live without happiness,' he once told his wife. It was more true, perhaps, that Pyke was one of those men whose essence denied them happiness, whose restless spirit rejected the tranquillity that happiness brings.

Yet happiness of a kind came to him at Cambridge, a town and university for which he cherished a life-long affection, even when, as he considered in later years, it let him down. It was at Cambridge, as a student, that he made some of his vast circle of friends who were to sustain him in his future projects, who were to support his school by sending their children to it and who came to his aid when things went wrong. Their loyalty never wavered.

Late in September 1914, Pyke, signed on by the *Daily Chronicle* as a foreign correspondent and armed with an American passport that belonged to a dead U.S. sailor, set off for Berlin. The intention, as it had been described by Pyke to the newspaper, was that, for a contract of £700 a year, he was to act as their contact during the war. But the tall, gaunt Pyke was captured almost immediately, and spent 112 days in solitary confinement before finally being interned at Ruhleben, near Charlottenburg. It was from here, after a nearly fatal attack of double pneumonia, that he made a spectacular escape to England, and wrote a book about his adventure.

Soon after his return, he tried to get back into journalism and was attracted to the *Cambridge Magazine*, a radical and, in some respects, unpopular weekly journal which took a pacifist line in policy during the war. The *Cambridge Magazine* was edited by Pyke's friend C. K. Ogden, who, although he could not offer him an editorial post, made him the paper's advertising manager. .It was while he was involved in this work that, in March 1918, he met Margaret Amy Chubb, daughter of a Hampshire doctor, and married. Soon after, the *Cambridge Magazine* fell worse into debt and was forced to close, and Pyke, once again out of work, took his new bride on a tour of Italy and Switzerland before returning to England to seek a livelihood.

'I went into the City and spent a day watching men entering and leaving the Stock Exchange. All of them appeared ineffably stupid, and many of them were my relatives,' he told his wife. It was obvious that if they could be successful at the business of making money, then Pyke could be a triumph. So he decided to play the market.

He began by studying the commodity markets, looking for a system. He read the literature, talked to the experts, studied the figures and gambled. Above all, he came together with some economist friends at the London School of Economics and together with them prepared graphs, on large sheets of paper pinned to wooden boards, to show the fluctuations of several different commodities, studying the interaction of their prices. It was in these graphs that Pyke found what he was looking for : an apparently consistent correlation between the prices of two metals – tin and copper. Pyke became absorbed in his studies and speculations. Instead of working through one dealer, he began to use several, borrowing from one to pay another, creating capital out of bits of paper, amassing in the process larger and larger stocks of metals, only to sell them again on marginal fluctuations on the market.

It all appeared to work. Despite the fact that he was using blatantly irregular methods, his scientific analysis of the situation seemed to be paying off. Asked to describe his activities in later years, Pyke called it : 'Risk-bearing, insurance against deviation of prices.' Whatever it was, it was certainly profitable, and Pyke was soon several thousand pounds in credit.

The birth of his only son, David, in 1921, was a turning point. Conscious of his own neurotic tendencies, Pyke dedicated himself to providing his son with a childhood that would be free from trauma. It is worth recording, at this point, that despite all that subsequently occurred, he realized his ambition. Forty years afterwards, David Pyke could recall that 'one of the factors of my life has been a distinct absence of revelations. People usually find that some adult experience awakens them to an aspect of life previously closed to them; I have never had that. Everything was always open to me. There were no secrets, no fantasies.'

Geoffrey Pyke did not think much of the education system of his time. The Edwardian era, like the Victorian, considered that children were somewhat stunted adults, unformed appendages of their parents, who should always be clean, rather better behaved than their elders and normally silent. The principle of firmness, of insistence on a clear code of behaviour and a fixed procedure of conduct, was universally accepted. Pyke, who could be cold and distant with adults, rebelled against these attitudes. Professor John Cohen, a life-long friend, once quoted Pyke as saying :

18

the fundamental principle we should follow in dealing with children is to treat every child as a distinguished foreign visitor who knows little or nothing of our language or customs. If we invited a distinguished stranger to tea and he spilled his cup on the best table cloth or consumed more than his share of cake, we should not upbraid him and send him out of the room. We should hasten to re-assure him that all was well. One rude remark from the host would drive the visitor from the room, never to be seen again. But we address children constantly in the rudest fashion and yet expect them to behave as models of politeness. If the principle suggested is to prove effective, there must be no exceptions. One rude remark to the child would give the game away.*

Pyke's first inclination was to spend his own time educating David; travelling with him, providing him with new experiences, finding him playing companions. It soon became obvious that this was unpractical. The demands of his business were too great. So Pyke had a better, bigger idea : he would start a school for David, based on the beliefs he held – a school that would grow into a research institute and provide the stimulus for an entirely new approach to education, in which children would be free to pursue any interest and be stimulated to inquire into any question. Its basis would be scientific inquiry, in which children would not be force-fed dogmas that pleased their elders, but in which logic would be paramount and personal experiment and observation the keys to learning.

Pyke was concerned about creating minds that were free to observe and equipped to draw logical conclusions from their observations. For that reason, for example, he sought to give David a completely unprejudiced view of language ('Shall we call this thing a book?' is how he would seek to draw the child's view to the fundamental nature of things and words).

He believed in self-discovery, as much because it was the most efficient form of learning as because he considered all adults biased and mentally warped; victims of folk-lore and

*David Lampe, *Pyke: The Unknown Genius* (Evans, 1959), p. 211. This book contains a fuller account of Pyke's life, particularly of his activities during the war, than can be given here.

prejudice. Children, on the other hand, behaved like scientists, looking at things and drawing their own conclusions. 'Pyke ranks the scientist, or correlator, as he is fond of calling him, highest among human types,' wrote Nathan Isaacs in a personal memorandum in 1924. 'He does not want to make scientists, because he does not want to do any "making" at all. He does not set up his idea of what a child should be made into against other ideas; what he does is to set up the child against all ideas. He does not want to limit a child's future by his own any more than any other past. Moulds are wrong, whosoever they may be; and shaping is wrong, whatever it may aim at. That, at any rate, is the assumption of his experiment: he may hope it will lead in one direction rather than in another, but it is the experiment that must lead.'

It was these views that led Pyke to place his extraordinary advertisements in the *New Statesman*, and it was this same interest that led Nathan Isaacs to read them. Isaacs, the son of a Russian Jewish family that had fled from Warsaw to Basle, came to England at the age of twelve. He spoke no English, and for two years battled with the language and made an attempt to obtain a formal education before, at the age of fourteen, leaving school to go into business. He began as a junior clerk to a button merchant, but after a brief stay was offered a very junior post in a field that excited his innate scientific nature: metals. Isaacs had a passion for rare, difficult metals, and was to spend the rest of his life in the market for them, becoming Britain's leading authority in the purchase of tungsten and molybdenum, and the man who, during the Second World War, was responsible for British supplies of these vital materials.

Established in the City, Isaacs pursued his other great interests: philosophy and psychology. Together with a young economist whom he had met during the First World War – Lionel Robbins, later Lord Robbins – Isaacs went to lectures on the subjects. In particular he attended a series of psychology lectures given by the Workers Educational

Association and presided over by a young university graduate, Susan Brierley.

Mrs Brierley, having completed a highly successful degree course at Manchester University, and having spent a year as a research worker at Cambridge University, was married to one of her former teachers, the botanist Professor William Brierley. When she began her course of lectures for the W.E.A., she was immediately made conscious of the intense enthusiasm of the young Isaacs, who plied her with questions, argued incessantly, refused to accept her carefully reasoned arguments and kept quoting great paragraphs of German philosophical works at her. One evening, he turned up with an eighty-page essay based on her previous lecture. It was a strange kind of courtship, but it could not be denied. The two eloped to Austria, from where Mrs Brierley obtained her divorce and became Mrs Susan Isaacs. The Workers Educational Association, after earnest deliberations, felt that the behaviour of their young psychology lecturer was not of the sort to be sponsored by the Movement, and ruled that she should not be allowed to continue with her work. Instead, Nathan Isaacs brought his new bride to a flat in Hunter Street, and the dialogue continued in private.

It was in that flat that Isaacs read his *New Statesman* of 1 March 1924, saw the advertisement and felt that this was exactly the kind of task Susan should undertake. His wife refused to listen to him, dismissing the notices as the work of a crank. Her view that they were nonsense might have prevailed had not a fellow analyst, Dr James Glover, a friend of hers who had analysed Pyke a year ago, spoken about him to her. He encouraged her to apply for the job, and allayed her fears about Pyke. With great misgivings, she took his advice.

Pyke was a great scribbler. He seldom wrote complete articles, but covered pages with a spidery hand on which he jotted down his thoughts, and it was a number of these pages that he brought to the initial meeting between himself and Nathan and Susan Isaacs. He was gentle, amusing and enthusiastic, and immediately captured the support of Nathan. Later Nathan, writing an essay on the project, eulogized: 'Pyke is undoubtedly an educational genius!' Pyke was equally attracted to the Isaacs. 'If only we can get her,' he told his wife after his first meeting with Susan, 'we shall be all right.'

Susan Isaacs, recognizing an affinity with a man who wanted to give young children a scientific and educational background and freedom unheard of at the time, was more cautious. 'For one thing,' wrote Nathan Isaacs, 'she is nothing like such a generalizer as Pyke. For another, she would discount some of the more extravagant fervour about science. For a third thing, she would think it time that a little more interest were shown in the children now, as against their far-off future. A large element in her motive would always be the fact of the actual emotional warping which she sees children undergo in unsuitable surroundings, under mistaken or perverse treatment, etc., and from which she would want to save them....'

So they met again, many times, arguing across the table in the Hunter Street flat, until a plan of action was agreed upon. Pyke would finance the new school, and pursue its development into a proper research institute of child studies. He would seek support for it, but would not interfere in the educational activities of the school or the tuition of the children, who would be in the care of the director, Susan Isaacs.

With this apparently amicable settlement reached, and with prominent advisers like Sir Percy Nunn, Professor Helen Wodehouse and Dr James Glover supporting the venture, the two now went ahead to make public their views on The Malting House Garden School:

It is now generally agreed among educationists that the first six or seven years of the child's life lay the foundations of his physical, social and intellectual development. This has long been realized as regards diet and the hygiene of the body. The great importance of the earliest stages of social and intellectual development is only now beginning to gain due recognition. Recent educational and psychological research has, however, made it abundantly clear that all the main lines of character and of intellectual powers and habits are determined in these early years, and that this is true in a much more detailed fashion and a much more profound sense than has hitherto been generally admitted. The provision of the right environment and of sympathetic guidance for the young child is thus not only a matter of great desirability, but one that requires the most careful scientific method, expert knowledge of child psychology and wide educational experience.

A group of parents in Cambridge are making arrangements for the early education of their children, and in securing the services of Mrs Susan Isaacs they have the assurance that a long-felt want has been happily met.

The general purpose of the Malting House Garden School is to provide, under expert and sympathetic supervision, the fullest opportunities for healthy growth in every direction, so that each child shall be free to gain control over his own body and knowledge of the physical world, to develop his natural interests, individual powers, and means of expression, while living in a happy children's community, the conditions of which will lead to normal social development.

The school will be held in the Malting House Playroom, with free access to a large garden with open-air shelter, which will be used as much as possible in suitable weather, for the children's activities. There will be every opportunity for free movement; the development of bodily poise and control will be provided for by suitable educational material, and by games and songs and dances. Arrangements will be made for eurhythmic dancing as a regular part of the school activities. Gardening will be one of the children's occupations. There will be ample opportunities for rest. . . .

The mid-day meal will be carefully prepared under the direction of a dietetic expert, and the Directress will be in close touch with a physician. Careful observations will be made of growth in height and weight, and general physical development. Records will be kept, and reports given to parents at intervals.

Social development will be cared for no less than physical health, since the two can hardly be considered apart; 'naughtiness' being so often the result of nervous fatigue, and, conversely, any condition of emotional strain and anti-social behaviour reacting at once upon sleep and digestion and bodily habits.

The school will be a children's community, in which self-reliance, control, and habits of friendly cooperation will be naturally developed by the experience of a real social life, by the joint activities of the group in play and songs, games and dances, in the common occupations of the garden and the care of animals, in social intercourse at mealtimes, and in various forms of art and handicraft.

The most careful attention will be given to each child with regard to his emotional and social development, and every detail of the school arrangements will be considered with regard to this. The value of community life, as a means of ensuring free and normal growth, both physical and social, is, as Dr Montessori and others have shown, scarcely to be over-estimated. It has, therefore, been arranged that the school shall open continuously from 9.30 a.m. to 3.30 p.m. It is very much hoped that parents will take advantage of this opportunity of a healthy, free and scientifically planned environment for their children, and will allow them to spend the full six hours in the community. . . .

Intellectual development will be directed largely on Montessori lines [that is to say, stressing individual development]. The Montessori apparatus will be available for the training of the senses, and for assisting the child to understand space, form, time and number, so as to lay the foundations of geometry and arithmetic. Reading and writing will be prepared for by the Montessori material and method, and for the older children material will be provided which will enable them to master these processes and to develop self-reliant methods of work. The development of speech will be cared for; language as a means of thought as well as of communication will have full attention. The study óf Nature will be provided for in the garden, and in the care of animals and plants; drawing, modelling and painting will give means of knowledge, of control and of self-expression. There will ·be training in musical sensibility as well as in song and rhythm. In every direction, the material with which the children work will be scientifically graded so as to stimulate intellectual effort without strain, and to make possible the development of understanding, of control and of self-reliance.

The school will in the first instance be designed for children of $2\frac{1}{2}$ or three years to seven years of age.

The premises where this ambitious scheme was to take place was a rambling eighteenth-century building in Malting Lane, Cambridge, owned since 1904 by Dr Hugh Frazer Stewart, Dean of Trinity College and a lecturer in modern languages. Pyke first moved into The Malting House in 1923 and later Susan Isaacs described how the house was converted into a school :

The school met in a large hall, from which easy steps ran to the garden, where there was plenty of room for running and climbing,

24

for communal and individual gardening, and for various sheds and hutches for animals. The garden had two lawns, and plenty of trees, many of them bearing fruit. The large hall had a gallery with stairs at each end, and a low platform, on which the piano stood. The horizontal framework supporting the roof made excellent bars for the children to hang on or climb up to.

Besides the large hall, there were four smaller rooms, and a cloakroom and lavatory. Part of the cloakroom was used as a kitchen by the children; the gas cooker, and shelves and tables for crockery and cooking utensils were kept there. The large hall was used for general purposes, and for music and dancing. In the first year, one of the smaller rooms was used as a rest room, and another as a reading and writing room for the older children of the group.

Later on, one of the rooms became a quiet room for the older children, with shelves for the school library, and the general reading and writing equipment. One large room was fitted up as a combined carpentry room and science laboratory. (The children at one stage called this the 'cutting-up room', as most of their biological work was done there.) The third was a handicraft room, with equipment for modelling, drawing and painting; and the fourth, a quiet room for the smaller children, in which reading and writing materials suitable for them was kept, and movable tables and chairs. The school was attached to a house, in which the children who were in residence lived.*

It was to this school that ten local boys came on 7 October 1924. There was P.O., a fluent talker with a bright expressive face, whose father was a Cambridge don. This small child delighted in drawing, cutting out, building and modelling, rarely sat still long enough to complete anything, but ran about the rooms, laughing to himself. When he hurt himself, he never sought comfort from an adult or one of the children, but would run off, throw himself on the floor or the stairs, bury his face in his hands and sob bitterly. When recovered, he would come back with the others again, without a word about the incident.

There was the small American boy, who, Mrs Isaacs noted, 'is very delicate, has had tubercular glands and liver trouble.

* *Intellectual Growth in Young Children* (Routledge & Kegan Paul, 1930), pp. 14–15.

Suffers from night terrors and has shown some general nervous habits. Very excitable.' It was this boy who once went home and told his mother that he had knocked Timmy down flat. 'Is Timmy a big boy?' his mother asked. 'Oh, no, he's so small he can hardly stand,' was the triumphant reply. It was this boy too who, looking dreamily at his dinner plate during a school meal, remarked to no one in particular, while the other children's conversation flowed around him: 'I don't like dreams; they are horrid things,' and then added, as an afterthought: 'What's more, I never have them.'

B.D. was four years old that month, a slightly built child with a mobile, expressive face of whom Susan Isaacs noted: 'He shows more hatred in his expression than any child I have observed.' B.D. was inventive and agressive by turn, initiating new games and then moving on to destroy other children's models or threatening their activities. His opening remarks to a child were: 'I will kill you!' 'I will shoot you!' 'I will hit you in the face!' 'I will kill you blind dead!' 'I will throw you on the roof so that you can't get down!'

There was H.O., $4\frac{3}{4}$ years old, tall and well developed for his years, who was extremely short-sighted and whose most notable characteristic was 'the flitting nature of his attention. He did not consider any object, apparatus or anything else for more than a few seconds, and then rushed off to something else. This appeared to be, in large part, a general exploration of the new environment. There was clearly some excitement and very great interest.'

There was C.A., nearly four years old, tall and clumsy, whose first day at school consisted largely of fits of screaming, and who was also extremely aggressive. He was very possessive, and snatched sticks away from other children even though he had one himself at the time. He developed a habit of spitting at children, and for an early period was quite unable to cope with communal life.

Ph.W., who turned five that month, was the oldest in the group. He was large and heavily boned, but surprisingly responsive to music. Obviously bright, he enjoyed modelling, drawing and cutting out, and proved very clever with his hands. Like many of the other children, he was extremely possessive, with a slyness that made him suggest escapades for the others to perform and to be caught out doing.

R.W., $4\frac{1}{2}$ years old, came to school on his own from across the Fens. A strong, healthy, self-possessed boy, he had great energy that took the form of rather uncontrolled rushing about the school. He delighted in smashing things, and one day he broke four vases in succession, picking up the pieces and smashing them again. He also had a streak of viciousness, and once bit Susan Isaacs severely, but on another occasion showed touching concern for her when she admitted that, grown up as she was, she also could cry.

Then there was T.M., at $2\frac{1}{2}$ years of age the youngest, smallest child at the school. Tall for his age, fair, very independent and self-contained, he had the gift of endearing himself to adult and child alike. Having achieved a structure of bricks or boxes, he would beam with delight and announce to the world: 'Timmy made it!' Unusually sociable, he would, if he needed, say, a pair of scissors, collect enough for all the other children and pass them round with the explanation: 'Here are some scissors for you.'

The interesting point about these children, and others who came to the school later, is that on average they were unusually bright. Dr Evelyn Lawrence, who came to the school in 1926, tested them and discovered that they had an average I.Q. of 131, with a range from 106 to more than 140. At the same time, some of the children were deeply disturbed.

'It was sometimes said by outsiders, not by us, that the ten most difficult children in Cambridge had been sent to us,' wrote Susan Isaacs. 'This was an exaggeration, but there were six or seven who were justly to be described as extremely difficult, and one of these was on the borderline of pathology. These parents naturally expected one to work miracles with their children, and when this did not happen within the space of a few weeks, they then conveniently forgot that the children had been

27

unruly before coming to the school, and blamed the disorder upon the school.'

Some of these children had particularly intelligent parents, with their fathers holding academic posts at the university. Professor Sargant Florence, the economist, sent his son, Tony. The Cambridge philosopher, G. E. Moore, took his two sons. The grandson of Lord Rutherford and the daughter of Lord Adrian both attended The Malting House School. Two lecturers in physiology at the university enrolled their children. On the whole, these parents were friends of the Pykes and were in sympathy with the general educational aims of the school, and it is notable how many of them subsequently led their children through a similar educational pattern, from the Malting House to the local Perse School, and then on to either the recently founded Bedales or Dartington Hall, followed by either Cambridge or Oxford.

Other children at the school had less academic backgrounds. There was the son of the local tailor, and the child of the local bank manager. One or two children from overseas were included, and there were a few others whose parents hoped that the special arrangements at the school would solve their particular parental problems.

Of those who stayed for more than a few terms, four were later to become academic members of staff of universities, one a medical consultant, one a teacher, another an actor, one a child psychologist and another a broadcaster. Of the girls, one married a judge, another an economist, a third a doctor. The close ties that linked their parents – a common community, a common town, the same friends – were to continue to link many of their offspring.

But on 7 October 1924, when the first detailed notes were taken at The Malting House, they were simply small and often difficult children. What they found was a world that was both permissive and full of activity. Susan Isaacs, or Mrs I., as she was known to all the children, recorded their first impressions.

At lunch, R. took a second helping of egg. I asked him to give me some. He replied: 'There won't be any for you' and took it all.

Running into the garden D. hopped on one leg, imitating another child. He then remarked: 'I can do it. If my leg was broken I should have to walk on one leg, should not I?' R. found a spider in its web in a corner of the hen coop. Very interested. Several of the children ran to look at it. D. also interested, but refused to come nearer than several feet away. Showed definite signs of fear. Children doing plasticine made a large ball and threw it about. Ran up into gallery with it and threw it down. I returned it to them, calling their names in turn. This established some order. They responded and threw it back in turn.

Digging in sandpit, R. said: 'What colour is the sand?' I said: 'Shall we call it yellow?' He replied: 'What colour is it?' and I said: 'It is yellow.' He replied: 'Well, it is brown.'

8 October 1924

The children standing at the door watching heavy rain heard the rustling noise of the rain on the leaves and G. said: 'Perhaps it is God saying that he will punish us for doing things we shouldn't.' I played piano for them to run round and they asked for more piano music. Beads were threaded and the colour tablets done by some children.

14 October 1924

C. very aggressive. Turned tables over. Took soda crystals out of box, threw them on the floor and refused to pick them up. Children sat in canoe for long time.

15 October 1924

G. spent a long time on the cylinders and built with bricks. Later in the sandpit he made an 'underground' with sand, dug a deep hole and poured water in the hole, R. also joining in. D. and R. and other children joined in washing up after lunch. Janet came to lunch. D. took command of her, ordering her where to sit, where to put her hands, what to do and squeezing her very often.

16 October 1924

C. much more friendly and co-operative. More willing to put things away. G. brought to school a pair of pincers. D. very anxious to use them. G. allowed this for a little time. The flitting attention of H. very marked.

Had the bonfire in the garden. C. said: 'Let us make the flames high. Let us make them go up to the sky.' G. said: 'If you do that you will burn God.'

17 October 1924

The children having had much water in cans, I prohibited them having more. T. and two others came to the tap for more and I said no. T., passing out through the schoolroom, saw the four vases with flowers on the tables, and putting down his can, took each vase in turn, lifting the flowers out and pouring the water into his can, then coming out into the garden, saying: 'Timmy has some water now.'

C. took a stick and started to bang the table with it. He came to me and banged the table close to me, threatening my hands. Then he said: 'You do it also.' I replied: 'No.' Then he said: 'Why not?' So I took a stick as well and did it with him, and he laughed, and ceased to do it.

20 October 1924

R. and P. in garden, digging, found worms. P. said: 'Shall we put a worm down her back, so that it will bite her?' R., when he finds worms, says: 'I shall stretch them until they break,' and does this.

28 October 1924

Children climbed on top of shed, and C. and Ph. and then all spat vigorously to ground, and sometimes at each other. C. and B. also spat often in schoolroom – I always asked them to wipe it off.

29 October 1924

Children made aeroplanes and engines of plasticine, spontaneously suggested by H., and then ran round the room shouting with them. B. and C. later, and T. and D. together, and then D. and G. together played shopping, making their own shops and clearing them up afterwards. Used this for practice in counting.

31 October 1924

B., as on one or two previous occasions, hit me in anger. I tried passive resistance, but he went further, and hit me several times, hard, stinging blows with the open palm, and was gleeful when he thought he had really hurt me and 'made me cry'. The method of remaining passive did not appear the answer, as his pleasure in the feeling of power appeared to grow and no compassion was shown.

10 November 1924

Children always seemed to be putting one child or perhaps two outside the group. They say: 'Shall we bury so-and-so in the Castle?' 'Shall we kill so-and-so?' 'Shut him out!' or 'So-and-so cannot come into our shop!' or 'There are no so-and-so's in our Castle!'

B. was shut out of the schoolroom by the other children. In trying to get in he broke the glass in the door. Great excitement. At dinner time he broke a plate by accidentally dropping it with pudding on it. Children laughed heartily at what seemed to be a great joke. Later in the day he said: 'Shall we break the window again?'

12 November 1924

... In the afternoon Mrs O. remarked how very much improved H. was at home and wondered what I did with him at school!

13 November 1924

H. and B. found a hoe and with it broke up a piece of the garden path, saying that they were mending the road. Spent much time and interest on this. H. then chipped the bricks of the house and wall until I stopped him. They used an old tennis net as a fishing net, hanging it from the window and insisting that I, when out in the garden below, was a lady diver.

14 November 1924

B. climbed up the gallery railing as G. often does, with some qualms and hesitations, but with success and pleasure when successful. Ph., following R. and myself, drew freely and coloured. Cut out picture of a plant in a flower pot, which he called a 'red daffodil'. T., not wishing to go into the garden to join the other children's bonfire, made one himself of pieces of paper and cloth and plasticine.

21 November 1924

I was opening the skylight window. Ph. greatly interested and wished to do it also. Then all the children joined in. They repeated it with the blind over one of the skylights. Much interested in pulling it down and shutting and opening it.

In the garden H. and P. and B. had shut T. into one of the hen coops. He remained cheerful as I was near and I talked to him through the wire. Half an hour later, the same boys being now inside the coop, T. ran up and shut them in and fastened it triumphantly. ...

31

When I was in the lavatory, H. came and peered through the frosted glass, shouting: 'I can see her in the lav. I can see her combinations.' Great glee. Later, tried to turn up my skirt to see them again.

24 November 1924

In the garden, the children found a small dead rat. They called it a mouse. H., P., and B. said: 'It is dead' and ran about with it. I took it away for fear of infection. D. said: 'You will not hurt it, will you?' I took it down the other end of the garden and threw it over the wall. D. asked where it was. I said: 'I have put it down there.' He asked: 'You have not hurt it, have you?'

8 December 1924

G. had been told at home that he would not be coming after Christmas. When alone with him doing plasticine, I asked whether he liked coming. He said: 'Yes, but not when the boys hit me.' I said: 'But they have not hit you today, they do not often hit you.' He said: 'No, but they did once....'

Seeing the skylight cord swinging, H. suggested fastening an aeroplane made of bricks and plasticine on to the cord and swinging it. All the children wanted theirs fastening on. This was done in turns and the cord set swinging vigorously. The children shouted with delight, especially when the aeroplane broke and fell. This was done many times and again on successive days....

The first term came to an end at The Malting House, and Nathan Isaacs, reflecting on the bold experiment, wrote: 'The school is going well, and one only wishes one could hurry time, and see the children so free to choose, so surrounded by choice, so empowered to choose; to see what large choice they will make at last; what they will have learnt to know, what they will elect to do, who they will elect to be.'

Susan Isaacs looked back on the past term and the way in which the teaching techniques, and the various activities, developed. There was music, first introduced by playing the piano to the children and suggesting that they should run around: 'The piano was a Grand, and the opening of the front to raise the support for the music directed the children's attention to the structure of the instrument and to the inside. They became more interested, for the time, in the mechanics than in the sound, and climbed on the chairs and on the piano itself to look at the wires and hammers. They all watched the hammers strike the wires, as I played, for a considerable time, and would take turns at striking the keys and producing the effect. There was some squabbling over the best position to see the hammers; but, on the whole, quite a useful experience in mechanics.

'They became more interested in the sound as the term went on, and the feeling for rhythm and the delight in moving differently to the various rhythms played developed very definitely and clearly.

'On several occasions, songs were suggested to the children, but these were never very successful, nor held their interest for very long. They would, however, join in the chanting. . . .'

In the early part of term, baskets, dishes, cups and saucers and jugs were made out of plasticine. Snakes were very popular, but some of the children also made more ambitious models of engines, trains, motor buses, goats, canoes and a long, jointed 'snake', with many of the children joining pieces together. 'Seeing me make several circles of different snakes, Ph. asked for a very large one, which he helped to make, and then called it a gramophone record. Then he constructed the whole gramophone, and sung the tune from the record. A telephone first made by P. or Ph. was used by all the children, who shouted down the phone : "Are you there?" '

The children were also introduced to number work. Although it was largely incidental to other, more practical activities, they counted the number of swings they had, how many of them were staying to lunch, shells, counters and beads in their 'shops'. The Montessori equipment – blocks, cubes, beads – was used every day, as were other materials such as that for sewing, a blackboard and chalk, scissors, paper, pencil and pens, and modelling wax.

But it was the garden, with its sandpit, trees, tools, canoe, hammock, hen houses and watering cans that captivated the children most of all. While the weather was fine – and it was a good autumn – they spent most of their hours in the sandpit, or brushing up the fallen leaves for the numerous bonfires in the grounds, or using the hollyhock canes as flags and poles, marching round the garden and singing. Towards the end of term, a separate plot of garden was arranged for each child, with its name written on a tab and stuck in the plot, each child being given some bulbs to plant. They picked wheelbarrows' full of pears from the trees and brought these to the house for the next day's dinner, or they would simply rush out into the garden to look at a passing aeroplane, and then dash back inside to model the plane in plasticine.

The children would have their rest period during the day, when they either had a story or slept. Some developed the ability to rest only towards the end of term, and for most of the time the children turned these periods into another game, dragging their blankets around the room by holding them in their teeth and biting them, or jumping from one to another. They also developed a number of standard games, such as 'shopping', with each child having its own 'shop' which was visited in turn by Mrs I. Occasionally, one or two of the children would pretend to be bad men, come to knock down the other children's toys or put them into prison, and towards the end this fantasy play developed into dressing-up and pretending to be Santa Claus.

Throughout the course of that first year at The Malting House, Susan Isaacs noticed a marked contrast in the general social feeling of the whole group of children. 'With the exception of B., the individual aggressiveness of the children has grown much less, the pleasure in co-operative occupation and the application of the simple rules insisted upon very much greater, the most striking instance being the rule that one set of material must be put away before another is brought out. At the end of the first term all the children appreciated this and rarely refused to comply with it.'

It had been a difficult start, but the situation looked encouraging. Geoffrey Pyke, normally in his dressing gown, was keeping his word not to interfere in the daily running of the school, and was rarely seen by the children, but stayed in his own study, surrounded by his mounted graphs. Nathan Isaacs, at work as a metal merchant in the City, commuted each day from Cambridge. At the start of the project, Pyke had offered him a salaried job keeping the school records, but Isaacs, although enthusiastic about the experiment, refused, on the grounds that he disapproved of Pyke's business methods and would not accept payment from such a source. It was not until a year later, when Pyke inherited some £9,000 from his relatives, and he approached Isaacs again with the offer, saying 'Now you cannot refuse me. This money is absolutely pure', that Nathan Isaacs gave up his London job and joined his wife full-time at the school. The contract that Pyke drew up between himself and Nathan on 15 September 1926 was an extraordinary one. It guaranteed Isaacs £500 a year, for four years, to write a number of books on the theory of knowledge. Pyke was later to explain that 'Nathan was told to run away and read and write. He had to research for four years and if, at the end, he produced, let us say, something useful, all the better.' The outcome of this opportunity was Nathan Isaacs' long essay, 'Children's "Why" Questions', which was subsequently published as an appendix to his wife's volume *Intellectual Growth in Young Children*, and which, at the end of his life, he maintained was his single most important published work.

Susan Isaacs, leaving the organization of daily affairs to Margaret Pyke, had her hands full with both the care of the children and the key task of recording their activities. Already her notes were filling out to make the basis of her subsequent theoretical studies, but she was aware of the great difficulty of trying to do both tasks at once, and appealed to Pyke for more help. What was required, and provided, was a set of shorthand typists, who would simply record, without taking any role in the affairs of the children, their daily activities and conversation, to provide a unique record of children in the act of growing up.

Not everybody approved. Cambridge, to which Pyke had

35

turned as a centre of enlightenment, proved to be as insular, as parochial and as opposed to educational adventures as any other small town. Stories about the activities at the scandalous Malting House grew over the coffee cups, until, inflated with distortions, exaggerations and sheer lies, they blew through the community on a wind of gossip. It was said that the children were put through tests of endurance; that they were made to climb trees and, once up, had the ladders removed to study their resourcefulness. Or they were being forced to crawl along the length of a high wall without any help. One of the most common stories was about a child who travelled to the school by taxi. The Malting House was so permissive, it was said, that when the boy refused to get out of the taxi, he was allowed to remain in and was driven round the town for the rest of the day, his father receiving a huge bill at the end of it.

These tales were probably helped along by incidents like that which occurred one afternoon when five-year-old David Pyke was taken to tea at Newnham College, and, tucking into the cake, announced to the startled ladies present: 'You have no idea of the smell inside a dogfish!'

(David Pyke was keen on dissecting animals, and once wrote to the London Zoo, asking them to send him the next animal that died so that he might examine it. His mother wrote a following letter, explaining: 'The animal in question was required by a group of children who are engaged on very elementary dissection for anatomical research purposes, and the letter to you was something in the nature of a social experiment to discover how dead animals could be procured. If by any chance it is the custom of the Zoological Society to dispose of animals that die, we should be very glad to know of this, and if this is so I should be very glad if you would give some indication of the cost. Perhaps you would also give me some idea of the frequency with which death visits the inhabitants of your Gardens. . . .')

'You have to remember,' one of the parents recollected years later, 'that, at the time, the idea of the school was considered pretty remarkable. What was most unusual was for parents to

think that children of that early age needed any kind of schooling or special attention – it was just that the climate of opinion
at that time tended to consider this irrelevant; people just did
not think of it.

'But the school, when you arrived in the mornings to bring
your child, was certainly not a bear garden; it was just an
ordinary, lively place, with some children playing. One didn't
get the impression of anything particularly unusual or dramatic
happening. It was just fun.'

The inability of a large section of the community to credit
the school with any of its real success was described by Susan
Isaacs in another way : 'In the early days, when the children
were more often anti-social, this was attributed to the methods,
or lack of methods, of the school; it was said that we "could
not manage them". In the later stages, it was on several occasions said to us : "Oh, of course, you have such an easy problem. Your children are so exceptionally amiable." '

Cambridge society was unconvinced at such protestations. A
famous phrase that went the social rounds summed up the
town's views. It was, they said, 'a pre-genital brothel'.

That was not how the children saw it, nor, many years later,
how they remembered it. 'I recall vividly my meeting with
Geoffrey Pyke,' said one, now a Cambridge don. 'I had something on my mind and I decided that I must discuss this with
him. I went to his room and asked if he would talk to me. He
said he would, and we began a discussion which went on and
on. It was an intensely enjoyable experience for me, and I
remember thinking, as I left, what a marvellous conversation
it had been. I quite forgot about the initial problem.'

Another pupil remembered that 'it all just seemed great fun
at the time. I do remember climbing trees, and, in particular
helping pour molten metal into a cold bath and watching it
turn into different shapes.'

'One of the best things about the school was that you could
make your own clothes, spend the day doing it without anybody telling you that you had to do something else, and then
change into your new clothes and wear them on the bus going

home,' said another who spent some years as a pupil at the school. 'Something that was very exciting to me was the stories which we used to dictate to Mrs I. She would take them down on a typewriter and then let us have them to take home. I remember both Mrs I. and Geoffrey Pyke as very quiet people. They were always encouraging but never interfering or shouting. One of my clearest impressions is that at the school we were encouraged to order our own meals. We used to have to decide what we wanted to eat, and then we had this written down on paper and passed to the kitchen. For a whole fortnight we had roast lamb, peas, roast potatoes, mint sauce and loganberries and cream! But on another occasion, we forgot to order, and then we got nothing except some fruit.'

Not everybody connected with the school held quite such glossy memories of it. Of that same incident, another observer, Miss Mary Ogilvie, who was a junior housekeeper at St Chad's, the house where the boarders stayed, also retained strong memories. 'It seemed to me to sum up some of the weaknesses of the school. You must remember that I came to The Malting House having worked with boys in the East End of London, and while I did not possess all the theoretical knowledge that the staff of The Malting House had, I had lots of practical experience of dealing with children. The staff believed that it was revealing of children's behaviour to try and make them order the meals themselves, and when they forgot, as they were bound to do, to give them only apples and oranges. This happened time after time, and of course, being small children, they often forgot. I felt that the experiment went on for too long, as did another one concerned with seeing whether children would tidy up by themselves. Well, of course, they didn't, and all that happened was, after a while, that they did not use the room that was untidy at all.'

These particular criticisms – of standing aside in the name of science and refusing to become involved in the confused world of childhood – were not lost on Susan Isaacs, and in her writings about the school (nearly all of them unpublished) she often came back to making a defence of her position. It was in 1926 that she first set out a detailed argument of the methods used at the school, in which she dealt with these points.

'The key to the school is the growth of the children, and its methods must be based on direct observation of the children themselves,' she wrote. 'One of the most far-reaching changes of thought in human history is the modern view of the freedom of children as the basis of education. This is the great experiment of our age.

'Merely to give a vague and general freedom is, however, not enough. We must also observe what children do under free conditions, and study the laws of growth, so as to be able to meet their needs in detail.

'The children are free to explore and experiment with the physical world, the way things are made, the fashion in which they break and burn, the properties of water and gas and electric light, the rain, sunshine, the mud and the frost. They are free to create either by fantasy in imaginative play or by real handling of clay and wood and bricks. The teacher is there to meet this free inquiry and activity by his skill in bringing together the material and the situations which may give children the means of answering their own questions about the world.

'This is our view of the function of the school, and this leads us to follow a heuristic method over the whole field of our children's relation to the world, particularly in the earliest years. Our experience has, in fact, led us to reverse the usual assumption which says either openly or implicitly to the child: "First learn what we have to teach you, then you will be able to do things for yourself." We cannot, in fact, teach him to grow, either in body or mind. Recent experimental work has shown, for example, that we cannot *teach* concepts of number to young children; these come by reason of the children's growth and concrete experiences of the world and we cannot hasten their coming.' (Susan Isaacs and Geoffrey Pyke were in close touch with the psychological child studies of Jean Piaget, in Geneva, to whom this is a reference. It was Pyke who organized Professor Piaget's first visit to England just as it was

Pyke who sought out the famous analyst Melanie Klein to analyse his son, David, at the age of three.)

'We can, however, at a later stage teach, for example, higher mathematics; in other words, the children's own natural ripening and immediate discoveries come first, and ability to profit by instruction comes later. We cannot do more than provide rich opportunities for early development, both because we have far less means of knowing what is going on in the minds of children in the earliest years than we have later, and because language, which is an essential part of instruction, is unsuited for the communication of knowledge and experience until these later stages are reached.'

Through this kind of criticism and discussion, the aims of the school were clarified, strengthened by daily practice, and tempered by experience. The school had taken on more children, and a mass of documentation on their daily conversations and actions now existed. By the beginning of 1927 all seemed set fair. Moreover, Pyke's dealings on the metal market were still proving profitable. There had been one nearly disastrous episode, when a short holiday on the Continent had coincided with a series of fluctuations in the market and some heavy dealing in tin and copper, but on his return a paper deficit was made good and Pyke once again moved into surplus. But it was becoming harder, and the fact that the profits were all on slips of paper might have made a nervous man pause. Pyke, however, assured his dealers that 'he would stake his hat on it', and everyone knew that Pyke did not wear one.

One of the applicants for a post at the school was Dr Evelyn Lawrence, who had just completed an economics degree at the London School of Economics. She received no reply from The Malting House, and instead went off to the Institute of Industrial Psychology, where she learnt about intelligence testing and modern techniques of interviewing. It was only then that she received a letter from Susan Isaacs, asking her whether she was still interested in a job at the school.

She was immediately won over by the charm and friendliness of both the Pykes and the Isaacs. In particular, she was fascinated by her interview, which bore no relation to the sort of techniques she had been studying. They all talked about her work and the school, and Pyke casually put on a record of Mozart, wondering if she knew what it was. She did. Immediately she was offered a salary of £600 a year, paid, twice a year, in advance.

Evelyn Lawrence's first impressions of The Malting House were favourable, but she was aware of the difficulties. 'The child psychologist has not yet completely formulated, much less solved, his problems. One of the reasons for this is that, under the old coercive methods of education, it was almost impossible for adults to know the minds of children. A few parents or teachers may have known their children well; but the number with both the inclination and the psychological training to describe them scientifically is lamentably small. It was felt, therefore, that an indispensable preliminary to improvement in educational theory was a detailed and consistent study of a group of children living under conditions of maximum freedom. This study is being made, and at the same time innovations in educational practice are being made and tried out.

'For the practical educator, there are two problems. To begin with, however much he may want his human plants to flower freely, and nature to take its course, however much he wants to break bad precedents and keep his new generation away from the shadow of the past, he knows that many courses are open to him, and that his choice will probably affect the whole lives of his pupils. He must therefore decide what kind of people he would like to produce. Secondly, having made this decision, he must find out how to get the desired results.

'The kind of people that the promoters of this school want to produce will have a scientific attitude to life. They must have intellectual curiosity and vigour, and be averse to taking their opinions ready-made. They must also be as physically healthy as possible. I think this is as far as Mr Pyke (I use his name merely as representing the group) would go in detailing the aims. He is anxious that the decision as to what exactly the children should become should arise naturally from the children's own characters, aptitudes and inclinations. Capacity for successful adjustment in society is included in the scientific attitude. Social ability is largely an intellectual thing, and if we can create reasonable people a large part, at least, of their social battle is won.

'The emotional life of the children makes an even more difficult problem. Our chief concern is to produce a new generation less nerve-ridden than the old. The newest psychology has taught us something about what to avoid in the way of repression, what kind of attainments should be encouraged, what sort of emotional outlets should be provided. This knowledge is being acted upon as far as possible, and new light looked for from the observation of this group of children.

'The best way to prepare a person for life is to give him a zest for life. The Malting House children certainly have it. When I first came to the school I tried to decide what was the most striking difference between this school and any other I have known. I came to the conclusion that it is the happiness of the children. Not that I have not been in happy schools. But I have never seen so much pleased concentration, so many shrieks and gurgles and jumpings for joy as here. Of course, this joy is particularly apparent because its expression is not hindered. If you want to dance with excitement you may. But even if the contrast is made with a free home environment, the distinction remains.

'I suppose the reason for this happiness is that there is plenty of space, that material equipment is abundant and suitable, and that the child is free to use it in ways that appeal to him, instead of being forced to do with it those things which his elders consider good for him. It is delightful to be in a school where the usual answer to the question "May we do so-and-so?" is "Yes" instead of the almost automatic "No" one finds oneself expecting.

'The consequence of this policy is that many activities which all children love, but which are usually indulged in when the Olympians are safely out of the way, go on in the school under the full eye of Olympus. These children play with water and

42

with fire, they climb and swing and even smoke, with the grown-ups not indulgently turning a blind eye, but approving and helping. As a result, these games are robbed of the fictitious charm usually given them by the need for conspiracy, and those in which this was the only support die out. For example, D. has a pipe of his own, but does not smoke it. Activities such as climbing and playing with fire, which contain an element of danger, are carried on in the presence of older people who can make sure that accidents do not occur. . . .

'. . . Discipline is very free. There is no punishment, and little admonition. Prohibitions, when unavoidable, are of particular acts, not of whole classes of conduct. It is not true, however, that the school is entirely without rules. It is generally understood that material used shall afterwards be put away. If the user (as often happens) is reluctant to clear up at once after his game, he is allowed to wait until he feels more inclined. But the matter is not forgotten, and sooner or later he usually agrees to put back what he has used in its place. Another rule is that implements must not be used as weapons. If this happens, the weapon is gently but firmly taken away. No anger, however, is ever shown by the teacher. If the two participants in a serious quarrel are unevenly matched, there is intervention on behalf of the one who is at a disadvantage, so that the weaker child does feel that he can get just support.

'There are three main advantages of freedom of action and emotional expression. In the first place, you can get to know your children. Under the old disciplinary methods, the educator knew his pupils only very partially and mistakenly. The child was forced to wear a mask of seemliness and respectability in the presence of grown-ups, and behind that mask his own inner life bubbled unseen. Here the children's crudities, the disorder of their emotions, their savagery even, are allowed to show. Emotional troubles can then be dealt with scientifically, or allowed to straighten themselves out, as they so often do, given time.

'Secondly, the danger of driving strong emotions underground to work havoc in the unconscious is avoided. The open expression of sexual interests is allowed, but where possible they are canalized by being turned into scientific channels. This freedom entails a certain amount of unpleasantness for the grown-ups. It is useless to expect children to be free at times, and at others to exercise discretion in situations where discretion is usual. But one cannot have it all ways, and it is time conventional parents learnt that their children are not the little angels they had believed. Hostility, another uncomfortable passion, is allowed freedom of expression. If the Malting House children hate a person, they tell him so. It is then possible to investigate the reason for that hatred, and probably to remove it. Fights and squabbles often occur, and if the fighters are fairly evenly matched, they are left to work out the adjustment themselves.

'This leads me to the third advantage of freedom. With conventional discipline, the child is kept wriggling under the dead weight of adult disapproval and prohibition. Here his position is that of a fencer, continually adapting himself to the shifting conditions of the group mood. This is what he will have to do in adult life, and it is surely a mistake to make all his social adjustments for him until adolescence, and then pitch-fork him into the world to discover from the beginning how human relationships work. When you have fought with an-other person over a thing, you realize that his desires are as strong as your own, and also, eventually, that fighting is not the best way of settling differences. The result of this policy in the school is not anarchy. I have seen several children combine to prevent conduct which they rightly considered unjust, and I have seen children of the most forcible character voluntarily submit to the leadership of a weaker-natured child.

'The position of the teacher in such a school as this is not an easy one. He, too, needs the alertness of the fencer. He must see immediately the implications of every remark, question, and act of the child, and respond appropriately with no appearance of indecision. He must possess unlimited patience and self-control. In fact, to support him in, and possibly lessen, the running fire of criticism he has to bear, the virtues of an arch-angel would come in useful.

44

'The second main function of the school, that of providing source material in the field of child psychology, entails the keeping of detailed notes. The children are under trained observation out of school hours as well as in them. In fact, there is no break between their school and out-of-school life. Practically all that they do, and much of what they say, is recorded. The children are discussed individually, and the meaning of their actions, as well as how to deal with them, considered. Much very valuable material has already been accumulated.

'My criticisms of the school are not so much criticisms as perplexities. In the first place, I do not know how much importance to attach to the factor of habit. We hope that the good habit of independent actions and intellectual curiosity will stick through life. May not bad habits, which the children are forming now, also persist? I should say that, compared with the ordinary strictly-trained child, these children have less self-control, worse manners, noisier voices, more selfishness. May they not injure their vocal chords before they learn to talk quietly, and build up habits of petulance and inconsiderateness which they will find difficult to break later on?

'We distrust the old conventional moral code, because it went so badly wrong in matters of sex. It is possible that we may make the mistake of throwing overboard with it much that was good. We probably still believe that kindliness, unselfishness, sensitiveness to the things that remain unexpressed but are important in other people's lives, are qualities of which the world cannot have too much. How are these children going to be won away from the "each for himself and the Devil take the hindmost" attitude? How are they going to see the value of giving more than a quid pro quo? They will certainly learn the minimum of agreeableness which will make them tolerable in society. Where are the works of supererogation coming in?

'Probably the answer to these questions is that the virtues I have mentioned are refinements, and that it is absurd to expect anything so difficult from people so inexperienced in life. At adolescence, they will possibly blossom spontaneously. At any rate, I personally am willing to wait and see.'

45

With the school now well established, Geoffrey Pyke was impatient to turn it into the Institute of Educational Research that he had always intended it to be. So he decided to advertise the wares of the school in a number of ways. First, he would comb the world for the kind of science specialist who would, specifically, bring his discipline to bear on the education of young children. Secondly, he would advertise the school itself and find it more supporters beyond the narrow circle of Cambridge friends who already subscribed to its principles. In an additional effort, he would have a film made to demonstrate to the public the practices already established at The Malting House.

In *The Times* of Tuesday, 26 April 1927, there appeared the following statement, across three columns :

W A N T E D – A S C I E N T I S T of the first order, if necessary of senior standing, but as young as possible, with a knowledge of the theory of science, to investigate and conduct the introduction of young children, $4\frac{1}{2}$–10, to science and scientific method.

The advertisement, which announced that Professor Sir Ernest Rutherford, Professor Percy Nunn of London University, and J. B. S. Haldane had agreed to help choose the successful candidate, went on to explain, in typical Pykian terms, what was required :

The ability to absorb instruction depends on the emotional attitude of the child towards the process of being instructed, as well as on the inherited quality of the brain. But the discovery of the idea of discovery and the ability to tolerate fact – which constitute the scientific attitude of mind – are the intellectual basis, on which, together with the emotional factor, subsequent intellectual progress is likely to rest.

Thus arises the need for a technique to utilize and develop the child's native curiosity in the way the wheels go round – his interest, for instance, in mud and water and his pleasure in messing about – in such a way as, in the long run, to obtain the maximum conversion of these drives into a controllable instrument of organized thought.

This involves the investigation by careful and delicate observation not only of what sort of activities are best introduced into the environment but what should be the order of opportunity for these activities. Much is done by leaving the child who prefers modelling with clay to heating mercury, or working a lathe to watching caterpillars or painting a table, to do so. But there is no such thing as absolute freedom and the very nature of the opportunities to a large extent limits and dictates his activities. And it is always possible – and this cannot be decided by *a priori* argument but only by observation – that to sip hastily at every flower may spoil the appetite.

It will not be plain that this type of environment-arranging needs also the provision of specially designed apparatus. Apparatus for adolescents is too arbitrary and traditional often in the very irrelevance of its forms, is insufficiently diagrammatic, and being designed for illustration and the support of textbooks and teachers rather than for discovery requires – as experiments on intelligent but innocent adults will show – a pre-knowledge of its purposes. The apparatus needs to be specially adapted to the child's capacity for inference, patience and manipulation, and to be designed to meet the lack of assumptions which are implicit in our adult thinking but, in haphazardly collecting which, a lifetime may be consumed. There is needed a continually accumulating fluid collection of apparatus suitable for each stage of the child's mental growth, devised clearly enough to enable him to discover in response to effort the answers to his own questions. Further, there is needed the verbal apparatus of explanations of the history of men's thoughts and instruments concerning the same problems with which the child is occupying himself; accounts receding further and further back into the past as the child's sense of a past matures, instead of an isolated 'subject' being worked uneasily forward to an ill-patched join with the present.

It is as yet uncertain whether there exist any special factors limiting or making undesirable the introduction of children of 4–10 to scientific knowledge and thought. That is to say, whether the apprehension of multiple and permissive causality which is painful to the human mind, with its innate tendency to accept and manufacture explanations in terms of unitary and magical causality, is in early life so much more painful that the forces – equally innate – of curiosity and intellectual aggression towards the external world would be stunted intead of stimulated. Or whether, on the other hand, it is not rather a quantitative question, as at present seems indicated – one of developing methods compatible with the child's childishness, with his need of phantasy, and of grading the demands of reality to his capacity.

This is the main theoretical question.

As it is hoped that the occupant of the post will, in addition to exercising and developing an art, make of the task a piece of scientific work and research, leading eventually to the publication of his results – negative as well as positive – he will need to make ample records. For this purpose the services of a shorthand-typist will be placed at his disposal.

Certain preliminary work with children of 4–7 has already been done at Cambridge at The Malting House School successfully enough to encourage the directors of the school to make a full-time, long-period appointment specially for its development.

They hope to make of the appointment the beginnings of a research institute into problems connected with education. Hence they are all the more anxious to obtain the services of someone of outstanding suitability for the work.

He would need not merely to be a specialist in his own branch but to have some little acquaintance with other sciences, the history of science and the history of religious beliefs. . . .

This advertisement, or edited versions of it, appeared in a large number of journals, including the *New Statesman*. It was also submitted to *Nature*, the only general scientific journal then being published in England. But it was refused. 'If ever the history of the school comes to be written,' Pyke noted in a letter to his close friend, Sir Percy Nunn, 'these two episodes ... should certainly be included.'

The incidents to which Pyke referred go back to 1924, when *Nature* accepted the original advertisement seeking a director for The Malting House. The owner of *Nature*, Sir Frederick Macmillan, of the Macmillan publishing family, was at the time an old man of between eighty and ninety years of age. He was struck by the unusual wording of the advertisement, and subsequently believed that somebody had told him it was a cover for an agency dealing in the white slave trade! When, therefore, *Nature* received the 1927 advertisement, and Pyke's name arose again, the doors were hurriedly slammed shut.

Pyke was both baffled, amused and furious, and in an intense campaign rallied all his considerable forces in counterattack. First he went down to London to see Sir Frederick. But when he arrived, the old man had left for home. Pyke stormed back to Cambridge and wrote letters to both his solicitors and advertising agents, asking them to confirm his personal standing with the publishers. Then he had another appointment to see Sir Frederick, and on his return wrote to his old friend, Percy Nunn.

It is an amazing story, though I hesitate to add further to your post in writing to you about it. He actually took seriously the suggestion that the advertisement of three years ago was one for the White Slave Trade, and when the present one was offered to *Nature*, out of lethargy and a desire for a peaceful life, he thought that it would be better to have nothing to do with it. His memory about the matter he admitted to be hazy, but he had, he confessed, the impression that there was something odd and unusual about it.

I have had considerable trouble in getting him to see me, and I do not think he likes going back on his previous decision. However, in the face of such a suggestion, even dating from his very first thoughts, I referred him on the one hand to my solicitors and on the other (without further asking you for your permission) to you as I felt confident I could do so.

His memory of the past is entirely confused; he is under the impression that someone wrote to him that by permitting the advertisement to appear in *Nature* he was allowing an international gang of white slavers to make use of the estimable pages of *Nature*...

Sir Percy Nunn wrote back immediately. 'I was about equally astonished and amused at your communication of the reason why *Nature* jibbed at your advertisement,' he said, and offered all possible help. Then Pyke sat down to deliver his final blow. He wrote to Macmillan :

Dear Sir Frederick, I have to thank you for sparing me so much of your time. You will perhaps forgive me if I put into writing a re-iteration of the statements I made to you, not only about the scientific standing of the Malting House School, but as regards my own personal integrity and moral position.

49

The Malting House School: 1924–9

The Malting House School was founded by me in 1924; the lady appointed to the position then advertised was a married lady, Mrs S. S. Isaacs, formerly Susan Brierley, one of the Assistant Editors of the *British Journal of Psychology*, whose textbook on psychology is published by Messrs Methuen; the advertisement now issued has no purpose beyond that which is carried on the face of it.

I should like to refer you as regards my own position to Messrs Blyth, Dutton, Hartley & Blyth, of Gresham Road, Old Broad Street, one of the oldest firms of solicitors in the country, who have known me for some years and my family for three generations; also to our mutual friend Mr Sullivan, to whom I was introduced by Lady Dorothy D'Oyley Carte, whom I think you also know; also to Mr Otto Kyllman of Messrs Constable, who some years ago published my book *To Ruhleben and Back*, and who has also known my family; not least to Professor Percy Nunn, Principal of the London Day Training College and Professor of Education at the London University, who is not only personally acquainted with myself and the members of the staff of the school, but who takes the keenest interest in the work. Likewise, I can, if you wish for further references, refer you to Messrs Langton & Passmore, solicitors, of 2, Paper Buildings, Temple.

In addition, I will, if you desire, ask Professor G. E. Moore, the Editor of *Mind*, whose two children are at the school, also to write to you about my personal standing, and if you wish for yet a further reference on this particular point I will explain the moral issue raised to Sir Ernest Rutherford, President of the Royal Society, whose grandchild is at the school, to give you similar reassurances. I write without previous reference to him, but I think it probable that both he and Professor Cyril Burt, Psychologist to the London County Council, would give you their opinion as to the probability of my being engaged in any improper purpose with reference to this advertisement.

I may mention that Professor Nunn, who was curious as to why the advertisement had not appeared in *Nature*, has already offered of his own free will – since he has not the privilege of your acquaintance – to speak to Sir Richard Gregory. I should also be prepared to ask Professor Nicholson, Professor of Physics at Oxford, to guarantee my respectability.

Though I appreciate that they are anxious to obtain as many advertisements as possible, I nevertheless am inclined to think that a paper of the standing of *The Times*, the *Spectator* and the *Observer* would not either deliberately or out of desire for advertising revenue, or even out of carelessness, accept an advertisement which could lay them open to the merest suspicion of countenancing anything not of the highest respectability. This reminds me that I should also be prepared to refer you to Mr J. R. Scott, of the *Manchester Guardian*.

My reason for availing myself of your kindness in listening to what I had to say is the slight that its non-appearance in the pages of *Nature* puts upon me in the eyes of the scientific world. I may add that I have not yet met one of my scientific friends since the advertisement appeared who has not asked me the reason for its non-appearance in the only general scientific paper.

I greatly trust, therefore, that despite the trouble to which I have put you, you will see your way to reviewing the decision of the Advertisement Manager.

Should you by any chance ever be in Cambridge at any time, I should be delighted to show you the working of the School and introduce you to the scientist for whose appointment the pages of *Nature* will, I trust, be responsible.

Pyke had his fun, and his victory. Two days later, a letter arrived at The Malting House:

Dear Mr Pyke, With reference to your visit here on Wednesday and the letters which have passed between us, I now write to say that we have decided to insert your advertisement, if you still wish it, in the pages of *Nature*. I am giving instructions to the Manager to insert the advertisement, if it is offered again.

Regretting the inconvenience which you have been put to in this matter, I am, Yours faithfully, Frederick Macmillan.

One of the immediate effects of the nation-wide campaign for the school was that the Press decided that The Malting House was good 'copy'. 'The Press have been bothering me for interviews,' Pyke wrote to Percy Nunn,

but I am refusing them as I don't want any personal publicity. On the other hand, I am suggesting to them that if they care to commission articles on research in education, from people of the highest standing, with the School and the advertisement that has appeared and the one that is going to appear as the topical relevance, then I am prepared to give such people any assistance in my power. It has seemed to me that this is an opportunity for getting the Press to say to people that research in education is an important thing. The object that I have in mind is that it should thus be easier for County Councils and so on, who live in terror of criticism about wasting money, to secure complacence with expenditure on psychologists and educational research. The idea that there is any connexion between research and education is new as far as the public is concerned, and until it has become quite familiar to them, even if they know nothing about it technically, the expenditure of every penny will be grudged. . . .

This particular letter carried a footnote. 'The *Daily Express* thought it suitable to send as the representative to interview me about the School their Crimes Reporter.'

Another journalist who descended on the school was a freelance, T. G. Tibbey, who recognized the importance of what was being done. 'Here you have a fine hall, work-rooms, a carpenter's shop and a garden. But more distinctively, you have things – all kinds of things. The garden has a sandpit which can be flooded and a wonderful climbing frame, specially imported, where the children can be as agile as monkeys with little fear of injury. It has plants which, if you wish, you may dig up to see how they are getting on. Above all, it has animals, no end of them. And the children pet them and look after them and watch them and order them and, on occasion, bully them, just as the natural child will. Once one of the animals died and they wanted to know why. But how could you tell them in terms they would understand? And what is the worth of all those answers which cloak ignorance and burke inquiry? Here, the reply is "Let's find out", so that the children have grown used to looking for the answers to their questions. Thus, quite simply and naturally, the little dead creature was dissected. They learnt far more than the cause of death. On one occasion, when a calf's head had at last been successfully sawn open, one child's comment was "What a small brain!" to which a six-year-old scornfully added : "Well, he didn't use it much!"

'Curiously enough, parents and teachers alike have noticed that, with this outlet for the natural desire of the human child to "see the works", there has resulted a greater kindness to and consideration for living animals.

'Curiosity, the desire to know why, is instinctive; it has helped to preserve the human race. As such it peculiarly belongs to childhood, and we, as peculiarly in another sense, so often fail to satisfy it in any adequate fashion that it fades away into that measure of dull acceptance which betokens dull people. The curiosity of the child often spells difficulty for the adult, but here, at The Malting House School, an attempt is being made to utilize the driving force of curiosity for the development of thought and knowledge ...'

Mr Tibbey went on to comment about the pupils themselves: 'At present there are seventeen of them, their ages ranging from three to nine years. They are in the main unusually intelligent children of professional people in Cambridge, distinguished among children indeed by the quality of their parents. For these have had vision. They established the school to revive for their children something of the advantages of the larger families of earlier days. Thus the school embodies at present the equivalent of perhaps four such families. They believe that to live with, play with, even quarrel with other children – there is much education in a quarrel – is necessary for child development. They even believe in beginning young, several being under three when they first come.

'Is not this practical expression of their faith by these comparatively well-to-do parents a commentary upon the need for the public provision of somewhat similar facilities for the children of poorer parents for which the president of the National Association of Head Teachers pleaded in her presidential address last week?

'There are still authorities which refuse to allow children under five a chance to attend school, and in the whole of England there is only accommodation for some 1,300 little ones in nursery schools. These Cambridge parents at least are satisfied with experiment and having passed through three years of patient inquiry and learnt and gained much, they are proposing to extend the scope of their work.

'Founded as a day school, it is now proposed that the school shall become partly residential, at present for children from four to nine years of age. And, characteristically enough, having secured a remarkable response to their advertisement for a teacher, the directors are now advertising for parents. They are not cranks, nor is this non-profit-making school intended for cranks. But they wish to discover whether there are sufficient scientifically-minded parents, who, whilst desiring that their children shall eventually take a normal university course, believe that this can be attained both more efficiently and more happily by methods other than those of the usual course of school instruction.

'For not only do they believe that for many pupils this fails to provide any adequate body of effective knowledge, but also that the methods of its acquisition often tend to set up faults of temperament and of attitude towards life which account for many of its failures.'

Pyke was indeed out to expand the school. In yet another series of advertisements, he set out to make The Malting House better known and to attract a wider range of children to it, 'in the belief that quite possibly there exists up and down the country a substantial number of parents who, while anxious to avoid the emotionally determined efforts of cranks, are nevertheless dissatisfied with the overworked ignorance of the majority of our schools.'

In these same announcements, Pyke claimed that, in reply to his appeal for a teacher, he had received applications from

8 professors and university lecturers
13 workers in pure research
19 workers in industrial research
29 medical men engaged in public health and general practice
37 professional educators
40 with other qualifications
47 without any qualifications

It may well have been the case, but the fact was that on the short list of suitable candidates there were few who really met the need. On the top of that list was a thirty-six-year-old Russian-born teacher from New York called Richard Slavson. Slavson had been trained as an engineer, but had a great interest in education and a desire to pass on his own passion for structures, and the mathematical laws that governed them, to children. He had worked with children at Teachers College, Columbia University, and Professor Kandel, of the Institute of International Education at that college, sent a glowing testimonial of his credentials. 'I am a little terrified at American ideas of salary,' Pyke said in a letter to Percy Nunn, 'but you can probably confirm my impression that American teachers are less well paid than American dustmen.' A few days later a correspondent of *The Times* in New York spoke to Slavson on Pyke's behalf, and the young man, convinced that he was setting out on a great adventure as one of the founders of a vast educational research institute, set sail for Britain.

Pyke, however, was already immersed in yet another facet of his public relations scheme. He had engaged British Instructional Films Ltd, who specialized in making nature films, to make a documentary record of the school's activities. E. E. Warneford and E. W. Edwards, two skilled natural history photographers who had to their credit the discovery of X-ray cinematography, were entrusted with the camera work. The production was in the hands of a young woman, Mary Field.

'He told us exactly what he wanted and I got the impression that some of the activities had been laid on specially for us. For example, the children were dissecting Susan Isaacs' cat, which had just died, when normally they worked with frogs or dogfish. They all seemed to be enjoying themselves immensely, digging away at the carcass. Only the cameraman and I were present while this was going on, and I can remember him turning to me and saying: "It fair makes you sick, doesn't it!"'

'Then there was the bonfire. It was supposed to be an exercise in free play, but it got a bit out of hand. The fire spread and spread and reached the apple trees, and then it destroyed a very nice boat. Even Geoffrey Pyke was a little upset about that, and he seemed a very calm man.'

A number of strong spot and floodlights operated by a generating lorry were used in the production of the film, together with great lengths of cable that ran over roofs and across gardens, through windows and up and down stairs so that the children could be photographed in their ordinary environment. 'In all our experiences in photographing every kind of wild creature, not excepting cultures of bacilli,' said Edwards afterward, 'the problem of photographing children in their wild state proved the most difficult to tackle.'

The photography of this two-reel film took nine or ten days of constant work, as it was necessary to accustom the children to the presence of strange adults and even stranger machines. During this filming, Mary Field had a chance to observe Pyke, who took a close personal interest in the project. 'I got the impression that he was far more influenced by Susan Isaacs than she was by him. He always spoke of her with great respect, although she was not often there when we were making the film. I personally thought Pyke was rather confused in his thinking about children, and mixed up ideas from Freud and Froebel in rather a haphazard way. He paid for the film himself, and I don't think he ever gave a thought to how much it might cost him, or where the money was coming from.'

The film was a great success. Four or five hundred people were sent invitations to the preview at the Marble Arch Pavilion on Sunday, 24 July 1927. The correspondent from the *Spectator* reported:

For a short half-hour I watched children of from four to nine years of age having the time of their lives, wading up to their knees trying to fill a sandpit with water, mending a tap with a spanner, oiling the works of a clock, joyously feeding a bonfire, dissecting crabs, climbing on scaffolding, weighing each other on a see-saw, weaving, modelling, making pottery, working lathes – in fact, doing all those things which every child delights in doing. At Malting House School children's dreams come true.

The school is equipped with the most extensive apparatus, which will stimulate the natural curiosity possessed of every child. The system of education adopted here is based on precisely the opposite principles to that suggested by the old moral tale of Harriet and the matches. It is a system of education by discovery, aiming at the preservation of this precious gift of curiosity. At present there are

seventeen children at the school, some boarders and some day children, and it is hoped that they will continue their education there
up to university age.

No child is ever told anything that he can find out for himself. For
the very young children, at any rate, there are no set lessons. Reading, writing and arithmetic are learnt theoretically after their
practical value has been realized. For instance, the cook would
give notice if she were perpetually bothered with countless verbal
requests for favourite dishes (she will only pay attention to written
menus) and so the children must somehow learn to put their requests on paper.

There is no discipline. There are no punishments. Children may
hit one another so long as they only use their hands, but I believe
quarrels are rare and, though it seems almost unbelievable with the
unending opportunities which must occur, there has never been an
accident of a serious nature. The children are left to form their own
opinions, tastes and moral codes. After having seen this film, I came
away wishing with all my heart that my own dull schooldays had
been as theirs were, and that education could be made such an
adventure for every child.

Those who had been invited to the showings were equally
rapturous. Pyke and Isaacs received dozens of letters, one of
them even enclosing a cheque, which was returned, for the
'research institute'. Pyke sent one letter on to Susan Isaacs with
the laconic comment that 'it is encouraging to hear that the
writer is "ours in camaraderie for life's little ones". I think that
we ought to frame her letter alongside that of Miss —— who
was "in reverence of our holy aims".'

At last, The Malting House was news. Pyke's mixture of
shrewd publicity and showmanship had brought it to the attention of the world. American educationists wrote, demanding
details. Copies of the film were begged from Pyke, who refused.
Slavson arrived from New York, was given a two-year contract
at £850 a year, and although appalled at his first view of the
school, which was far from the mental picture he had carried
away with him across the Atlantic, set to work to prepare for
the new autumn term. The school was enjoying its high summer.

As always, the fortunes of the school depended on Pyke's ingenuity on the Stock Exchange. By February 1927, he had made about £10,000 on his dealings, and held considerable stocks of both tin and copper. But the Inland Revenue was pressing him for tax, and, to avoid this, Pyke formed two companies, to whom he sold his holdings. The companies, of both of which he was the principal shareholder, paid him a salary of £7,500 a year as 'financial adviser' and both were empowered to lend him sums up to £10,000.

But in the U.S.A., the copper trade was being welded into a giant international consortium to stabilize prices and eliminate speculation, and Pyke, speculator extraordinary, who at one time owned more than a third of all the tin and copper held by Britain, was one of the principal targets for the new combine. The metal market was preparing for a major showdown.

Of this impending battle, the Malting House staff was oblivious. When the school opened its doors again in October, the stenographers were in their places to add to the collection of records that now were piling up in volumes in Susan Isaacs' room. One secretary was specifically assigned to Slavson, and noted down the first experiments of the new recruit to the staff.

10.5 a.m.
J.A. comes in, and goes to middle bench where his aeroplane is resting.
'Ah, that's my aeroplane.' Then he turns to Mrs P. who has come in.
'What are you making?' He looks about and says :
'I want to make a shelf for my Daddy, yes, that's what my Daddy wants for his stamps.'
He then goes to the aeroplane and says :
'I can't imagine how this aeroplane breaks.'
He feels back wing of aeroplane which is very insecure.
Jack comes in.
'Where's Mr Slavson?'
He is told that he is through the house side. He dashes out to find him.
J.A. fits a piece of wood which has been used before into a wood vice, then takes a nail, and with a side stroke begins to hammer it

into this piece of wood that he has fixed into the vice. He continues to talk:

'Do you know what a nice aeroplane mine is?' He stops hammering and looks about. 'I'm, you see, I'm sort of making that hole, yes, that ...' and he again begins to hammer nail in.

Jack returns, pulling Mr S. by the arm, 'Come on, Mr Slavson, I'm the engine and you're the carriage,' and runs round Mr S. holding his hand. Dillon comes in, and in a friendly way lifts Jack up in his arms, and carries him out on to the landing; the latter appearing willing.

J.A. takes piece of wood out of wood vice, and puts it back in the wood racking, saying: 'I'm going to make something quite big, I want to ...'

Dillon and Jack return.

Jack: 'Mr Slavson, I want to make a French monoplane.'

Mr S.: 'You start.'

Jack: 'I know how to make it, quite easy.'

J.A.: 'I'm going to make something big.'

Dillon leans up against middle bench with a strip of wood in his hand.

Jack: 'Mr Slavson, have you got any long, square pieces of wood?'

Mr S. hands him a piece of wood with equal length and depth, and about six inches long.

Jack: 'That's just right'.

Mr S.: 'What would you like to do?'

Jack: 'I'd like to make an aeroplane, a huge one.'

Dillon: 'I can't see a piece of wood like that. I want a piece of wood like that.'

Mr S.: 'Do you want to come down with me and get some? John, do you want to come down with us and get some?'

J.A., Dillon, and D.P. go down with Mr S. to the cellar to fetch some more wood. ...

11.5 a.m.

D.P.: 'Mr Slavson, the axle has come off.'

Mr S.: 'Why, do you think?'

D.P.: 'Because of that nail' (pointing to bent nail).

Mr S.: 'What's wrong with that nail?'

D.P.: 'I don't know.'

Mr S.: 'Do you think it's long enough to hold that (axle) in place?'

D.P.: 'No, it's too short. ...'

12.5

Peter asks Hugh to put candle on the bunsen with some pincers.

J.A.: 'I'm making a coracle. No, a ship. The Nelson ship, Nelson's Victory. I have seen it in my engine book.'

Janet: 'I started mine long ago.'

Leslie goes around and asks J.A.: 'What are you making, a boat?'

J.A.: 'Yes.'

Janet says that hers is a sailing boat.

Hugh and Peter are again burning rubber and then put a live match in the air hole. They also push a lighted match inside the piece of rubber tubing and see it go out. The matches in the hole ignite.

Peter: 'Nice fireworks!'

Leslie and Ann D. still play with tubes and water.

Mr S. asks Leslie why the water goes up in the tube, but gets no reply. But when he nips the tube, Leslie says it does not go up because he squeezes the tube. . . .

Hugh and Peter are very pleased with the effect of a piece of rubber in the bunsen burner. There are three flames.

Peter asks if he may have a piece of wax about $1\frac{1}{2}$ inches cubed. He asks if he can have all of it.

Mr S.: 'All you asked for.'

Peter: 'We don't want a piece of glass.' He asks Janet to look, as the bunsen burner now has three flames, two out of the air holes and one out of the top . . .

J.A.: 'What a squeaky saw this is!' He is using a small cutting saw, and creating some noise with it as he saws.

Timmy, who is kneeling on the floor: 'It may be rusty.'

J.A. continues sawing, and after a few seconds says: 'This saw needs oiling very badly.'

Timmy: 'You have got the same saw as I'm using.'

J.A.: 'Mr Slavson, I want you, Mr Slavson.'

Mr S. walks over to him.

J.A.: 'This saw is squeaky. Where is the oil? . . .'

Mr S. gives him the oil can.

J.A. (to Janet): 'I'm oiling.' Begins to saw again, and says: 'Lots and lots of little beds I'm making for my animals . . .' (laughing).

These activities, so typical of the daily life of The Malting House, were suddenly and violently disrupted by events taking place in the study of Geoffrey Pyke. For in this October, Pyke had bought, through his companies, a large quantity of tin, at a high price at a time when the production of tin was outstripping demand. Now, according to his own principles of dealing, he ought at the same time to have sold his copper holdings. But Pyke, aware of the stabilizing influence of the American cartel, for once departed from his normal practice, an action which he later described as 'imbecility and commercial rashness'. The result was that his charts, so carefully plotted to relate fluctuations between the two metals, became meaningless. The price of copper began to fall, and with each hour Pyke's subsequent dealings in the metal depressed the price more. Whatever he did, he could only lose. By the end of the month, both his companies had lost all their assets, and the three brokers with whom they had been dealing were demanding payment for a total of some £70,000 or, by 1969 standards, a quarter of a million pounds.

When Pyke realized that, at any moment, his major creditors would take out judgements of bankruptcy against him to reclaim their money, he moved swiftly to The Malting House. From his office in London, he gathered together his personal assets and wrote £2,000 worth of cheques, sending them together with specific instructions to his wife Margaret in Cambridge.

On 1 November 1927 an extraordinary staff meeting took place at the school. In the evening, Margaret Pyke called everyone together and told them of the school's changed fortunes and of Pyke's determination to keep it going. To ensure this would happen, she explained, Pyke had made out their salaries for the following year, and during that time would seek to raise money to keep the school open. Then Margaret Pyke handed out cheques – £300 to Evelyn Lawrence, £640 to Richard Slavson, £300 to Miss E. R. Clarke, another teacher, £100 to Miss Ogilvie, the house matron, £100 to Miss Irvine, another teacher, and £40 to the cook, Miss Wilson.

It is impossible to say, at this stage, whether it was the news of Pyke's near-bankruptcy which persuaded Susan Isaacs to leave The Malting House. Certainly it was not the only reason.

Throughout 1926, Pyke had consistently been encroaching on her work, showing visitors through the school during sessions, arguing about the way the children were being handled, driving forward his own ideas of the school's future. When Susan Isaacs reminded him of their strict agreement that the teaching and management of the school would remain in her hands, Pyke burst out : 'Whose idea was it? Who got the money to start the whole scheme? Who initiated the policy of working with these children?' He accused her of openly stealing his theories of child education, of feeding on his genius. The way he had handled the appointment of Slavson also rankled with Mrs Isaacs, and the employment of a virtually inexperienced science teacher, who proved to have great difficulties in settling down with the rest of the staff, only added to her dissatisfaction.

There was also the inherent clash of two strong personalities, which the earlier experimental days had minimized, but which had since grown in sharpness. Pyke was a strong, quiet-spoken but dominant figure. Susan Isaacs, a Lancastrian, was both intellectually honest and shy, covering that shyness with a certain dogmatic attitude that brooked no change. Her husband wrote, after her death, that she had a deep, underlying lack of self-assurance which made her too readily fall into a defensive, fending-off attitude, because she could not really afford to have *any* defence breached.

'At the centre she felt too sensitive and vulnerable, and if she didn't preserve her outer defences intact, at bottom she knew that she couldn't and wouldn't fight,' he said.

She also felt a certain injustice in Pyke's attitude and his accusations, which daily grew more outrageous. Dr John Rickman, who wrote a long obituary of Susan Isaacs in the *International Journal of Psycho-Analysis* in 1950, gave praise to both Pyke and Susan Isaacs when he said of the school that 'our understanding of child development was given new data and our attention was challenged by the vigour with which it was placed – almost thrust – upon our attention.' But he perceptively added that it was due to Susan Isaacs that 'an extravagant idea was turned into a sober plan of action'. Susan Isaacs knew what her contribution had been, and was going to be, in the years to come, through her writings and teaching. Pyke, under mounting pressure from creditors and the Inland Revenue, was not prepared to be reasonable.

By the end of the year, Susan and Nathan Isaacs resigned from The Malting House and one of the main props of the experiment had been removed.

Other problems now crowded in. One of Pyke's companies, which could show only some £600 in assets and had incurred enormous debts, went into liquidation in November, with Geoffrey Pyke standing as guarantor for its losses. On 2 December, the second company also went insolvent, and it was only a matter of time before bankruptcy proceedings were instigated against Pyke, by now a sick man who more than once contemplated suicide, collapsed and left The Malting House for Switzerland to recuperate, leaving Margaret to sort out the wreckage. For two months, he remained inaccessible, only to return in February 1928 to try, even now, to salvage the school. For the sum of £451 14s., which included 10s. for the school's 'goodwill', he sold Malting House's furniture and oddments to one of the parents, Dr Edgar Obermer. This curious transaction – there was virtually nothing to buy – indicated as much as anything the intense devotion that the school had inspired in those who had supported it, for most of Obermer's money was, in fact, guaranteed by other parents and well-wishers, including both Victor Gollancz, the publisher, and Siegfried Sassoon, the writer. The boarding establishment, St Chad's, was transferred to Dr Adrian (later Lord Adrian, Master of Trinity College, Cambridge), who went to live there with his family. To all intents and purposes, the Pykes were now living as guests in premises in which they no longer had a financial stake.

Pyke, however, refused to give up all hope. In 1928 he wrote to the Laura Spelman Rockefeller Trust in New York, hoping for a grant to enable the school to continue its work. Pyke explained to the parents supporting the school that 'money is not the only difficulty which has to be reckoned with. Some of the staff have naturally to look to their own future, and two or

63

possibly three of them will be leaving this term. Substitutes for these will be obtained as far as possible, although they can be engaged only temporarily for one term. If the Rockefeller Trustees finance the school, by Christmas the position will, of course, be perfectly straightforward and the way clear both for the permanent engagement of staff and the expansion of the school as originally planned. ... May we, through this coming term, count on your willingness to leave your children with us? It is certain that without this support from the parents it will not be possible even to wait until the Rockefeller Trustees have had time to decide whether the school shall continue and develop or whether it shall be closed down and the work finally abandoned.'

Together with his application to the Foundation went a memorandum from possibly the greatest galaxy of academic figures of the day ever assembled for a private fund-raising scheme :

We understand that Mr Pyke is making an application to you for financial support in order to continue the work of The Malting House School, which is in danger of shortly coming to an end.

The school was founded in 1924 and has been financed entirely by Mr Pyke, who, convinced of the necessity for research work of this type, devoted to this and allied work the proceeds of inherited fortune, and, simultaneous with directing the school, entered upon a financial career in order to provide funds for its endowment and expansion.

Of the value of the educational work and psychological research which are being carried on at the school, we as a body are not competent to speak – but what is clearly the first requisite of scientific work, to wit, a copious and careful record of phenomena, is being kept to a degree which we believe, at any rate in this country, to be unique. Should these observations prove to be of the value they promise, they will provide a starting point for further research and also common data for discussion by anthropologists, sociologists, educationists and psychologists. Clearly also, any technique that may be evolved from such investigations should render the school valuable not only as a centre of research work but also as a training ground.

We further venture to suggest that your support of the effort that has already been made would have a yet wider significance. Science owes much to pioneers who have worked independently in the No Man's Land between the different sciences, until they have reached a stage at which they could command the support of established institutions. But many who have the will, insight and capacity to initiate such work must be deterred by the risk that the cost – always difficult to estimate – will exceed their personal resources before they have been able to prove the value of their research. Such men, we believe, would be encouraged to make the necessary sacrifices if they knew there were a possibility that if financial assistance were required to carry the work to a stage of proof, it might be forthcoming from Institutions such as yours.

Among the signatures to this dramatic appeal were those of Sir Charles Sherrington, Past President of the Royal Society, Professor Cyril Burt, Professor Jean Piaget of Geneva, J. B. S. Haldane, G. E. Moore, then Professor of Moral Philosophy at Cambridge, and Professor Percy Nunn. Altogether eight of the seventeen signatories were Fellows of the Royal Society.

What were these men trying to save? Dr John Rickman, who was later to pose the same question, suggested that there were two answers: a planned experiment in education, and one that took note of the phantasy element in the developing mind and personality of the child. But the school was more important than that. It broke entirely new ground. It demonstrated beyond dispute that young children could be treated with a freedom, civility and creative kindness which was hardly conceivable at that time. Moreover, in its meticulous note-taking, the school provided a body of systematic data on child development which was subsequently to form the basis for two of Susan Isaacs' most important books, *Intellectual Growth in Young Children* and *Social Development in Young Children*, which remain standard works to this day. Finally, the work started at Malting House, the work, that is, of setting child development studies on a proper, experimental basis of research and observation, was carried over to London University, where Sir Percy Nunn founded a Department of Child Development largely to harness Susan Isaacs' talents to the university. It was this department which, through the case material provided by Malting House, introduced thousands of student teachers to the developing minds of young children, and so helped to bring about the radical changes that primary education has undergone in Britain in the post-war years.

But the application was turned down. On 12 April 1928 Geoffrey Pyke was given a receiving order, and the final attempts to save the school which had, in all, cost him £15,000 of his own money, ended.

For the whole of that year, children still turned up at The Malting House, and the remaining teachers continued to make notes of their activities. But the numbers involved gradually diminished, and from a bustling school the character of the experiment gradually dwindled to that of a small, doomed community. On 5 May 1929 Pyke went into a nursing home, and two doctors declared a few weeks later that he was suffering from amnesia, paranoia, 'is dangerously ill and unlikely to live through the night'. The 'ferocity of purpose' with which he believed intellectual ideas should be pursued was, for the moment, at an end. At thirty-six, a period of his life had finished. A second chapter was to culminate in his work as a backroom 'boffin' in Lord Louis Mountbatten's Combined Operations Staff during the Second World War.

Following his suicide in 1949, a friend, Lancelot Law Whyte, described his particular gifts in this way : 'With Einstein there is his theory. With Whittle there are the jet planes howling across the sky. Pyke's genius was more intangible, perhaps because he produced not one, but an endless sequence of ideas, each of which in turn obsessed him passionately, and each of which was lit with the strange fire of his mind . . . Pyke's method was to approach any problem on the widest possible basis, taking as little as possible for granted, in order to find the best line of attack ... but enthusiasm has no staying power without encouragement. The point is that the more receptive a community is towards originality, the more it benefits. It did not encourage Pyke.' Professor J. D. Bernal spoke of him as 'one of the greatest and certainly the most unrecognized geniuses of the time.'

From the Malting House, Margaret Pyke sent out her last note to the few parents whose children stayed until the end. It was dated 17 May 1929 :

It has unfortunately been found impossible to carry on the school beyond the end of the current term. The exact date of the end of term will be announced later, but it will be during the last ten days of July, and the school will then be permanently closed.

The Burston Rebellion: 1914

*We came on strike because our Governess and Master were dismissed
from the Council School unjustly. The Parson got two Barnardo
children to say that our Governess had caned them and slapped
their faces, but we all know that she did not. Then our Governess lit
a fire one wet morning to dry some of our clothes without asking
the Parson. So the head ones said that our Governess and Master had
better be got rid of. ...*

Emily Wilby, aged ten

In the early part of the century, staff in elementary schools
were not expected to hold unorthodox views or to have gained
a reputation for originality. They were required simply to maintain a façade of social respectability and to obey the policy
decisions of their education committees and local managers,
who were appointed to carry out routine administrative duties
and generally supervise the work of the teachers. For the most
part the managers were solid and unimaginative citizens who
refrained from interfering in the day-to-day affairs of education
unless some renegade in the profession adopted an independent
line and showed signs of disloyalty to the Establishment.

In two cases where teachers came into conflict with their
managers, the differences of opinion were so fundamental that
parents took a hand in the disputes and declared their interest
by refusing to allow their children to attend school. At Dowlais,
in South Wales, the pupils of a Roman Catholic school came
out on strike in support of the managers, who accused the headmistress of assisting a non-Catholic candidate in the local elections. The situation had all the characteristics of a poor theatri-
cal farce except that the participants had no intention of giving
anyone cause for laughter. For over three months the school
was occupied only by the teachers, and the managers exerted
every conceivable pressure in an attempt to force the headmistress to resign. When she was unsuccessfully charged with
assaulting a pupil the police had to provide an escort to take her

home and a constable remained on guard outside her house. The local authority refused to dismiss her and the managers countered by demanding an investigation into alleged irregularities in her registration as a teacher. Twenty parents were fined five shillings each and ordered to send their children back to school, but not one of them obeyed the instructions of the court. A writer in the *South Wales Daily News* commented :

> The whole case has been a scandal, and has resolved itself into a simple issue as to whether a priest is to be allowed to deprive a teacher of her livelihood and to ruin her career for the flimsiest and most trivial reasons.

As it turned out, the answer was that a priest who was also chairman of a managers' committee *could* ruin the career of a teacher for flimsy and trivial reasons. The Board of Education held two inquiries. The first was favourable to the headmistress, but after the second the special commissioner from London attempted to reach a settlement by recommending that she should seek alternative employment or accept nine months' salary if she was unable to find a similar position elsewhere. The headmistress refused even to discuss the offer but in a high state of nervous exhaustion abandoned the fight and left for her home in Manchester. At the same time, the National Union of Teachers, still groping for recognition, admitted its inability to influence the case and threw in the towel. Normal educational service resumed at Dowlais.

That was in 1914, the year that another school strike attracted the attention of the national press. On this occasion the battle was centred on the tiny isolated village of Burston in Norfolk. The two cases were similar in so far as the teachers and managers declared open war, politics were instrumental in causing the dispute and the dominant church in the area was involved on the side of the managers. But at Burston, parents and children struck on behalf of the teachers and entered upon a long and tough campaign against the authorities. It was more than twenty-five years before the dispute was finally settled.

It was customary for the managers of Burston School to meet at the beginning of each term to consider routine matters of administration and policy. The agenda for 10 January 1911 was more than usually brief, and in normal circumstances the Reverend Doherty and his three farmer colleagues on the Board might have anticipated spending not more than an hour of their spare time discussing the education of the village children. But there was one pressing item – the appointment of a new head teacher – which could not be settled without a lengthy and heart-searching discussion.

The only application forwarded by the Norfolk Education Committee was from Mr and Mrs Thomas Higdon, who, until recently, had occupied the posts of head and assistant teacher at Wood Dalling, a small village fourteen miles outside Norwich. It was the customary practice for a rural school to be the responsibility of a husband-and-wife team, and on the face of it the Higdons were distinguished only by the fact that superior qualifications gave Mrs Higdon the senior position.

The Burston managers made no objection about that. Their reservations were chiefly about the political reputation of the candidates, who had left Wood Dalling under a thick red cloud. Apart from his school duties, Thomas Higdon was a local organizer for the Agricultural Labourers' Union, and a convinced socialist. At Wood Dalling, he had organized the workers' vote and ousted the farmer-controlled parish council in favour of candidates who represented the Democratic Labourers. They, in turn, elected Higdon chairman.

Inevitably, the schoolteachers made enemies, but the situation had been worsened by their attitude to the school managers, whom they regarded as political opponents. A series of petty disputes culminated in a complaint to the Norfolk Education Committee that Mrs Higdon – a woman whose thrusting personality outweighed her sense of discretion – had referred to the managers as 'liars'. She admitted describing as lies certain statements of the Board but, despite the advice of the National Union of Teachers, was unwilling to apologize. The Education

Committee then demanded her resignation but at the same time offered to transfer both teachers to a less turbulent village.

If the Burston managers were wary of employing such notorious agitators as guardians of their young, it must be said in defence of the Higdons that they held an´equal aversion to the councillors in Norwich. They would much have preferred to stay where they were.

Both sides succeeded in overcoming their doubts, the Burston managers because they desperately required a head teacher and the Higdons because they needed work. The Reverend Doherty had at least the comfort of knowing that he was soon to leave the area for a new appointment, and could hand over the responsibility for the welfare of Burston to an incumbent whose devotion to religious and political orthodoxy was matched by his determination to fight for his beliefs.

The Higdons arrived at Diss station on the morning of 31 January 1911. There was no one to meet them, and they set out to walk the five miles to Burston. They were a devoted, and in many ways eccentric, couple. Both subscribed to extreme egalitarian principles, but they enjoyed and positively sought the dominant, autocratic role in any activity in which they participated.

Their origins were obscure. Mrs Higdon was accustomed to a middle-class environment, and it was said that she was the daughter of a Somerset doctor. Her family connexions with the medical profession may have been deduced from her preoccupation with hygiene. Pupils in her school were regularly instructed in the therapeutic benefits of fresh air, cleanliness and exercise. She was a vegetarian, and although her husband did not share her culinary tastes he was required to abstain from a meat diet. In so far as she was well educated – she spoke several languages and had a passion for reading, as well as adoring children – Mrs Higdon was a natural teacher. She reserved for her pupils a spirit of generosity and kindliness which she seldom extended to adults, and she was particularly belligerent and tactless when she encountered those who regarded themselves as her social superiors.

Thomas Higdon's interest in education was marginal. He believed in the power of learning as an instrument to create social justice and equality. But, as time went on, he devoted less energy to formal teaching and concentrated more on the pursuit of his political ideals. George Thomas, General Secretary of the Agricultural Labourers' Union, recruited him as a local organizer, and his success in that capacity established him in the role of a public speaker and political pamphleteer. He had sprung from a family of yeoman farmers, and his knowledge and ideas were largely acquired by self-education. Along the way, he had earned himself an Oxford local certificate which qualified him as an assistant teacher, but his chief pleasure was writing, and his style was that of the popular nineteenth-century novelists who filled their works with emotional, homespun philosophy and frequent rhetorical appeals to the gentle reader.

The Higdons' first impressions of Burston were influenced by the circumstances that had brought them to the village. The houses were dilapidated and insanitary, there was not a single branch of the Agricultural Labourers' Union in the area and the wages were lower than in the Wood Dalling district (at that time, the average payment to a farm worker in Norfolk was 12s. 4d. a week). By Mrs Higdon's standards, the school could not be expected to function efficiently while there was inadequate lighting, heating, drainage and ventilation. To be saddled with such inferior facilities was a poor reward for her successful efforts to persuade the Education Committee to build a new school at Wood Dalling, and her hopes of achieving any improvements were dampened by the knowledge that Burston had employed a dozen teachers in as many years, and that both her immediate predecessors had applied for transfers after working in the village for less than three months. It is just possible that the new occupants of the school house were temporarily mollified by the Education Committee's plan to replace the worn-out furniture, and the managers' offer to spend a maximum of three pounds on re-decorating the school.

A month after the Higdons' appointment, the Reverend

Doherty's replacement as rector of Burston arrived with his wife and two teenage daughters. The Reverend Charles Tucker Eland was a strict churchman raised in the Victorian tradition. He was in his early fifties, and enjoyed the settled convictions of middle age. His attitude towards his parishioners was conditioned by his belief that God 'made them high or lowly and ordered their estate', and his purpose was to instil into them the understanding that respect for authority on earth was a fit preparation for the paradise of the life to come.

He inherited the undisputed right to lead the community. Most of the land in Burston belonged to a large estate, but there was no resident squire, and by virtue of his income and social standing the rector had the best claim to the loyalty of the village. Both he and his wife were automatically elected members of the Board of School Managers.

It was clear from the start that the representatives of church and school had nothing in common. Higdon, who later described the rector as a 'narrow-minded Church bigot and despotic parish priest', was strongly averse to any form of organized religion, and he made no attempt to hide his distaste for the established church. His wife attended Sunday services, but was soon deterred by Eland's rigorous opposition to the nonconformists, whose chapel he regarded as a citadel of evil.

For two years the Higdons maintained an uneasy relationship with the school managers. The head teacher regularly submitted appeals for extra facilities, and the committee reluctantly passed on her recommendations to the county authority. The most urgent problem was heating, and eventually, eighteen months after the Higdons arrived in Burston, the Norfolk Education Committee invited the managers to consider two alternative plans for improving the physical comfort of the children. They decided to fix ventilators in the windows, and to install a boiler in the cloakroom to heat the water pipes, 'provided that it is cheaper than an open fireplace'. When this financial proviso was satisfied, it was agreed that the work should be put in hand as soon as it was sanctioned by the Board of Education.

If for one moment the managers believed that their benevolence would be acknowledged with gratitude by the Higdons they were quickly disappointed. In the second week of December 1913, Mrs Higdon complained that, despite the new boiler, the walls in the boys' lobby were damp. Without seeking approval, she committed the cardinal sin of making use of the open fireplace to supplement what she regarded as an inadequate heating system. The managers inspected the school, found no trace of dampness and instructed the head teacher to reserve her allocation of coal for the purposes of stoking the boiler. Mrs Higdon ignored the order.

But before the committee was able to consider the best means of enforcing its authority, Thomas Higdon discovered a new line of attack. In March 1913 he was urged by members of the Agricultural Labourers' Union to offer himself as a candidate in the forthcoming parish council elections. The agricultural workers were slowly realizing their political strength, and, although the Union was loosely attached to the Liberal Party, its members were out of sympathy with gentlemanly leaders who disguised their Conservative principles with a thin veneer of radicalism. Socialists like Higdon were capable of attracting strong support in their local areas, and the schoolteachers' political campaign in Wood Dalling had already achieved for him a reputation for successful parish electioneering.

After two years of political abstinence, Higdon was unable to resist the appeal of leading the farm workers against their employers. The fact that two members of the existing council were school managers and that Eland was a candidate acted in no way as a deterrent. Higdon accepted nomination, and a sufficient number of his sympathizers were persuaded to stand with him, so that each sitting councillor could be opposed.

The annual parish meeting was held in the schoolroom, and the council, who invited Eland·to join them for the occasion, were seated on the platform. It is unlikely that they were ignorant of Higdon's intentions, but they showed no sign of anticipating defeat. Perhaps they were relying on the traditional election procedure – voting by a show of hands – which inhibited the timid and spotlighted the socialist agitator, who was open to subsequent economic and social pressure. The system had worked very well in the past, but on this occasion the council's expectations failed to materialize. All but one of the retiring members were defeated, and their chairman was bottom of the poll. Eland failed to be elected, an indignity accentuated by the announcement that Higdon had received more votes than any other single candidate.

From this time, the battle between church and school entered a more vigorous phase, and the village heard the first rumblings of what was later known as the Burston Rebellion. Mrs Higdon continued to use the open fireplace, and wrote to the Education Committee to complain of the parsimonious attitude of the managers. The managers, in turn, protested that she had no right to appeal over their heads and reminded the committee that '. . . the cold condition of the school . . . was entirely due to her own fault as she had unnecessarily opened the windows and had removed from one window a pane of glass.' The coming of spring and the warmer weather produced a temporary lull in the battle !

In May, Eland was elected chairman of the school managers. His first inclination was to pacify Mrs Higdon, and his committee agreed to purchase a wire rope for the school bell, and a larger water tank. Whitewashing and limited structural repairs were already in progress, and a motion to '. . . present Mrs Higdon with the wood taken from the cloakroom' was carried unanimously. At the same time, they turned down a request of her own for '. . . a scullery window to open outwards'. To Mrs Higdon, any concession was an open invitation to ask for more, and she reported that the lack of proper drainage in the playground had caused damp rot in the floorboards of the schoolroom.

Before the committee turned its attention to this new problem, the Reverend Eland left with his family for a holiday in Switzerland. During his absence, there was an epidemic of whooping cough in the village, and Mrs Higdon contacted the Reverend Charles Millard, rector of Shimpling, a neighbouring village, and vice-chairman of the Board of Managers, who authorized her to take any action she thought necessary. So the school closed for one week.

When Eland returned, he received a letter from the Norfolk Education Committee requesting the managers '... to consider the reduction of the holidays by a week to make up for the irregular closing of the school, and also to warn the Head Teacher as to the closing of the school for sickness in future.'

At the July meeting of the Board, which Millard did not attend, the epidemic was the main topic of discussion. Mrs Higdon was reproved for having taken action without permission, and a letter was drafted to the Education Committee pointing out that '... owing to the needs of harvest it was not desirable to shorten the usual [holiday] period.' Eland evidently believed that the head teacher had made him look foolish in the eyes of the Education Committee and his fellow managers. In early November, when he learned that Mrs Higdon was once again making use of the boiler and the open fire, he finally lost patience.

He wrote to the chairman of the Education Committee. 'As Mrs Higdon seems to wish to act contrary to the Managers' wishes, and has so many complaints to make as to the present building, the Managers ask the Committee if they will kindly remove her to a sphere more genial.'

The Education Authority was not prepared to act immediately on this recommendation. For one thing, the building inspector's report showed that the school *was* damp, and that extensive alterations were necessary before the drainage system could be described as satisfactory. But, nevertheless, Mrs Higdon was warned of the possible consequences if she continued to defy the managers. She must have realized that a second posting would endanger her livelihood, and she reluctantly accepted the decision.

It was no secret that the Higdons despised the rector and, for his part, Eland freely expressed his disapproval of the two schoolteachers and their principles. From his point of view, their not attending church set a bad example to the rest of the village, they were discourteous and insubordinate and their political affiliations set them in opposition to established authority. Even so, ill-feeling might not have degenerated into open and continuous conflict had not the managers unexpectedly discovered a powerful ally.

A few days before the end of the Christmas term, the Board interviewed a Mrs Philpot and her two Barnardo foster children, Ethel Cummings and Gertie Stearness. She alleged that Mrs Higdon had severely punished both girls when they had complained of the indecent conduct of one of the boys in the school playground. The managers listened to their statements and unanimously agreed that they were speaking the truth. The head teacher was invited to answer the charges, but refused to appear at the inquiry. Then she was informed by letter that the children would attend the school after the holidays '. . . and were not to be treated differently from the other children. In the event of any further complaint the matter would be reported to Norwich for the Committee to deal with.'

No one can give an entirely unbiased account of the events immediately following this extraordinary meeting. According to the managers '. . . on the opening of the school on the fifth [of January 1914] the mistress brought out these girls before the whole school, close questioned them day after day, kept them in during playtime with the object of making them contradict themselves and wrote libellous letters and telegrams to Dr Barnardo's Home concerning them and to Mrs Philpot with a view of having the children removed.'

The Higdons claimed that Gertie Stearness, who had recently joined the school, freely stated that she had witnessed the indecent conduct of a boy *before* she arrived in Burston. In any case, said Thomas Higdon, the boy in question had been absent on the day the offence was supposed to have occurred. The teachers admitted sending letters to Dr Barnardo's Home, stating that Ethel Cummings was mentally and morally defective and a danger to the school. They denied having beaten the children and blamed the foster mother for the ill-treatment they had received. Mrs Higdon demanded an impartial inquiry, and

78

the Education Committee, after requesting a detailed report from the managers, set up an investigatory panel headed by the chairman of the Norfolk County Council.

It was clear that in the village there was strong support for the Higdons. But politically and socially influential friends were hard to come by, and even some of those who automatically ranked as sympathizers hurriedly disclaimed their connexion with the rebel teachers. For example, Herbert Day, treasurer of the Agricultural Labourers' Union, believed the allegations, and even representatives of the National Union of Teachers found it difficult to admit that some of the wealthiest and most powerful members of local society would deliberately engineer a plot to rid the village of an eccentric schoolmistress and her husband. They had to agree, however, it was strange that until Mrs Philpot's accusation the managers had shown no interest in the Barnardo children, who were poorly dressed and slept in a small, damp, low-roofed room.

The N.U.T. wanted to avoid an official inquiry and sent down an adviser, who urged the Higdons to come to terms with their employers. 'Keep smiling on the managers,' he cried as his train moved off from Burston platform. Later, Mrs Higdon received from the N.U.T the draft of a letter she was supposed to send to the Education Committee, assuring them she had not punished the girls excessively. The communication was never posted.

Legal assistance was reluctantly provided, but Mrs Higdon was warned that the Union executive was '. . . relying absolutely upon your statement that there is nothing *whatever* which would be proved *detrimental* to yourself in relation to your treatment of the children in question. *Under these circumstances you must of course accept full responsibility for the results of any such inquiry.*'

The tribunal was in session for two afternoons during the last week of February 1914. Mrs Higdon was ill, and did not put in an appearance, but she was represented by the N.U.T. standing counsel. On Monday, her lawyer cleared her of the fire-lighting charge. It was introduced by the managers to re-inforce their plea for her instant dismissal, and their failure to secure the expected verdict gave them cause for concern. The inquiry was adjourned until the end of the week, and during the interval Eland called in a Norwich solicitor to act for the managers. On Friday, the tribunal considered the allegations of Mrs Philpot. Subsequently, Thomas Higdon claimed the N.U.T. counsel grossly mishandled the case. He refused to call witnesses, arguing that they were to be held back for a possible slander action; failed to cross-examine the two witnesses put up by the prosecution; and made it known that, in his opinion, the letters to Dr Barnardo's Home contained language that was difficult to justify. 'He gave up the fight,' wrote Higdon in disgust.

In the circumstances, it was not surprising that the findings of the tribunal were unfavourable to the schoolteachers. The members unanimously agreed :

1. That the Head Teacher has been discourteous to the School Managers;

2 (a) That in view of the direct conflict of evidence with respect to the caning of the Barnardo children ... they are not able to give a decision in this matter; but they are strongly of the opinion that there is no evidence that Ethel Cummings is mentally and morally deficient or a danger to the School as stated in the letters of the Head Teacher and her husband;

(b) That, in their opinion, these children are well-treated and cared for by their foster-mother, and that the children are not afraid of being beaten by her;

3. That, in their opinion, the communications sent by the Head Teacher and her husband to Dr Barnardo's Institution were not warranted by the facts of the case.

The tribunal recommended :

1. That it is in the interest of Elementary Education in this village that the Head Teacher should seek other employment with as little delay as possible.

2. That, no punishment book having been kept in this school by the Head Teacher prior to this occurrence, she be directed faithfully to keep such a book.

Three years later, when Burston was the national centre of an educational and political crusade, the National Union of Teachers held its own inquiry. The lapse of time, the difficulty of persuading witnesses to attend and the mass of conflicting testimonies added to the complications of the case, but after ten meetings the committee arrived at some interesting conclusions. They found that the principal witnesses were no longer prepared to accuse Mrs Higdon of ill-treating her pupils. Even the rector skated round the issue, and, since there was no previous record of the schoolmistress resorting to corporal punishment, the committee ruled that she did not cane the Barnardo children. Moreover, while Ethel Cummings may not have been 'mentally and morally deficient' she was, according to this committee, 'dull and subject to lapses of memory'. But most important, the N.U.T. argued that, irrespective of the rights and wrongs of Mrs Higdon's professional behaviour, the manner in which the County Council inquiry was instituted and conducted made their report totally invalid. In the first place, Mrs Higdon did not attend the proceedings. Secondly, the letters to Dr Barnardo's Home, copies of which Eland was somehow able to obtain, were inadmissible evidence. Finally, the rector was too much involved in the case, as he had acted both as plaintiff and judge when the managers carried out their preliminary investigation. The Union also admitted that the assistance and advice offered to the Higdons was inadequate and blamed the members of the Law and Tenure Committees, who were jointly responsible for defending the interests of the schoolteachers and yet were unwilling to cooperate efficiently or act decisively.

These findings represented a *volte face* on the part of the N.U.T. executive. But in the spring of 1914, Union officials were pre-occupied with the task of implementing the recommendations of the County Council inquiry with as little fuss as possible. Mrs Higdon's brother travelled to London to meet the central N.U.T. executive. They agreed a letter should be sent from the County Association to the Education Committee, expressing the hope 'that she [Mrs Higdon] will not be unduly pressed, but that she may be afforded ample time to look around and secure a suitable and congenial post.' When Thomas Higdon got wind of the surrender terms, he reacted fiercely, and wired his brother-in-law to demand a 'fight to the finish'. His request was granted, if not by the N.U.T., at least by the County Council, which offered Mrs Higdon three months' salary and her husband one month's salary in lieu of notice, and instructed them to find alternative accommodation in the space of two weeks. The order was dated 31 March 1914.

On that day, the people of Burston discussed a plan of action. At first, the Higdons were not consulted, but they were probably aware of what was happening. Certainly by the end of the afternoon they were left in no doubt of the villagers' intentions. A boy scrawled across his exercise book : 'We are all going on strike tomorrow.' The same message was pinned on the notice board in the school porch and the signpost at the village crossroads, and it seemed appropriate that the rector's gate should be similarly defaced. Violet Potter, a fourteen-year-old pupil, collected the names of those children whose parents were ready to support a demonstration of unity. All but seven signed the declaration.

That evening, the parents held a meeting on the village green. Their leader was George Durbridge, a local fish hawker who supplemented his income by regular poaching expeditions. He was distinguished from most of the other working-class villagers by two notable characteristics : he made no secret of his political allegiance to the Conservative Party, and, every Wednesday, after spending his illegal earnings in the public houses in Diss, he beat up his wife. His free-booting activities were brought to a violent end in 1920, when his eldest son defended his mother by the only means at his disposal and dispatched George Durbridge with a blast from his own shotgun.

But in March 1914 Durbridge was able to perform a useful social function by organizing the village to protect their schoolteachers. The meeting was a huge success. There were cheers for the Higdons and boos and hisses for the rector. A resolution calling for a public inquiry and a school strike to last until justice had been seen to be done was passed unanimously. It was dark when it all ended and the last speakers stood in the glare of the oil lights on Durbridge's cockle stall. 'Stick like glue!' he shouted as the crowd dispersed into the gloom. They gave him the biggest cheer of all.

A temporary head teacher, who was also a member of the N.U.T., arrived the following day. The rector and several policemen watched as nearly sixty children gathered on the village green and formed up for a procession. On the first chimes of the school bell, they moved off, carrying banners with the slogans 'WE WANT OUR TEACHERS BACK' and 'JUSTICE WE WANT'. Young Violet Potter played the concertina and led the children on a tour which ended at the post office, where the proprietor handed out glasses of lemonade, nuts and sweets. The procession was repeated in the afternoon and each day for the rest of the week.

The strike was a popular diversion for the children, but they were not allowed to escape entirely from the routine of normal school work. The Higdons continued to give lessons, at first on the village green and later in a temporarily vacant cottage. They even took advantage of the free loan of a coal-shed and a copper-house. While circumstances may not have favoured the efficient teaching of mathematics or science, there was no difficulty in encouraging the children to compose exciting essays based on their unusual experiences. Emily Wilby, a ten-year-old pupil of the Burston Strike School, expressed the convictions of many parents and children when she wrote :

'We came on strike because our Governess and Master were dismissed from the Council School unjustly. The Parson got two Barnardo children to say that our Governess had caned them and slapped their faces, but we all know that she did not. Then our Governess lit a fire one wet morning to dry some of our clothes without asking the Parson. So the head ones said that our Governess and Master had better be got rid of. They had their pay sent and two days' notice to leave the school. Governess did not know we were going on strike. She bought us all some Easter eggs and oranges the last day we were at the Council School.'

The Higdons refused to leave the school house until the County Council served them with an eviction notice. They fought a last-ditch battle in the Diss Magistrate's Courts but the J.P.s ruled that payment of salary discharged the local authority from the obligation to allow the usual three months' notice to quit. On the day of the eviction – one month later than the original terminating date – the village turned out with carts and wheelbarrows to help move their furniture and the school-teachers accepted an offer of lodgings in the mill house.

The school managers were still not entirely convinced that they faced a serious attack on their authority. Eland described the strike as 'a nine-days wonder' and prophesied that the children would soon return to their proper school. He forgot to take into account the journalists of the popular national newspapers and magazines, who gave wide coverage to a human story of the little man's fight against autocracy, and strengthened the determination of the strikers by transforming Burston into a focal point for socialist pilgrimages.

Each Sunday, crowds of visitors arrived in the village. They came to see what all the excitement was about and stopped to listen to political speeches and to participate in religious services conducted by Free or Primitive Methodists. On one occasion, more than 1,500 sympathizers joined in a demonstration and procession. Three hundred and fifty of them were members of the National Union of Railwaymen, who travelled from all the main centres in the south of England. 'Their banners looked lovely,' wrote a young observer, '. . . they were all floating in the air beside the green fields and between the hedges and trees.' Two brass bands, one from Norwich, the other from London, headed the march, and George Edwards, vice-president of the Farm Workers' Union, delivered a sermon based on the text: 'Thou shalt not bear false witness against thy neighbour.'

The Burston Rebellion had all the characteristics of a classic melodrama, and by common consent the rector was the villain of the piece. He and his church were held responsible not only for the unjust dismissal of the schoolteachers, but the misfor-

tunes and poverty of the entire neighbourhood. His congrega-
tion dwindled to about half a dozen stalwarts. When sighted
by the audience at an open-air political meeting, he was chased
through the village and compelled to take refuge in the church.
There was a marked increase in the number of weddings and
christenings at the nonconformist chapels, but the rector held a
monopoly of the local burial facilities, and with reluctance his
parishioners continued to patronize the cemetery. Even so,
Eland was not permitted to conduct the graveside services, and
only once was he able to submit a successful claim for burial
fees. The boycott was a constant source of embarrassment and
remorse to the church officers. After the funeral of an elderly
Strike School supporter, the sexton was overheard to reflect
sadly : 'This old man lay here and he ain't paid for.'

Eland was not left entirely without friends, though, and the
County Education Committee retaliated on behalf of the school
managers. Eighteen summonses were taken out against parents
who refused to send their children to the state school. They
appeared before the Diss magistrates, and the strikers made
political capital of the occasion by organizing a procession to
the court. The Bench made allowances for what they described
as a 'not unnatural feeling on the part of the parents and children', and though each of the defendants was fined half-a-crown
the proceedings were characterized by the good humour of the
participants.

'Have you any reason to give?' asked the chairman, when
Thomas Mullinger admitted his son was absent from school.

'No, only he was on strike, and he dare not break the rules.'

'Nor must we break the rules,' said the chairman. 'You will
be fined two shillings and sixpence.'

A fortnight later, another batch of summonses was issued,
and thirty-two parents were fined five shillings each. The money
was raised at the Sunday meetings, and since court action
appeared to be serving no useful purpose the Education Com-
mitee abandoned this line of attack.

Encouraged by the school managers, the wealthier residents
of the village resorted to a more ruthless but traditional means

of asserting their authority. The Higdons had acquired a disused carpenters' shop for three pounds a year, which they converted into a classroom. The property was let by Ambrose Sandy who, in turn, paid rent to Mrs Ford, wife of a local farmer. In late 1915, she served on him an eviction notice and took possession of the cottage and the shop. Her action attracted a good deal of adverse publicity, and indirectly strengthened the case of the Burston strikers. Ambrose Sandy was blind.

Three glebe tenants were also evicted, and in two cases force had to be used by the church authorities before they were able to gain entry. One of the families had lived in their cottage for more than eighty years. These incidents prompted the Higdons to embark on a heavily emotional propaganda campaign. They wrote a stirring pamphlet addressed to the 'Men and Women of Britain' and called it *Prussianism in Norfolk*.

At the present time, when our brave soldiers are fighting Junkerism abroad, the little village of Burston in Norfolk is being goaded beyond measure owing to the tyrannical action of the village glebe owner.

The Reverend Charles Tucker Eland, Rector of Burston, and owner of 54 acres of land, is trying his utmost to hound and evict bravehearted men, women and children from the land of their fathers.

These folk owe no rent, they are good and true citizens, and their sole crime is that they have dared to elect the local schoolmaster and five labourers to the Parish Council in preference to the reverend gentleman and five farmers. ... The reverend gentleman is determined to pursue the poor folk with relentless animosity, evict the parents and break up the school.... two ... men are threatened with eviction in Xmas week. ... BOTH THESE MEN HAVE SONS FIGHTING IN THE TRENCHES, while the reverend gentleman is trying to break up their homes.

The Bishop of Norwich has been appealed to, and he advises them to go to law. But, whilst the Bishop lives in a palace and has an income of £4,500 per year, the agricultural labourers, working long hours daily, cannot indulge in such luxury as law. The Hon. Arthur Henderson has been appealed to ... but nothing effective has yet been done.

Will you who may receive this leaflet help us by writing to

your Member of Parliament, or by bringing this dreadful injustice before your Trade Union or Trades Council quickly? Get these bodies to adopt strong resolutions and send them to the Premier, the Home Secretary and the President of the Board of Education. Thus you can help to avert the calamity which has come upon these unfortunate villagers.

A few days later, Thomas Higdon was summoned for riding a bicycle during the day without lights. He refused to pay the half-crown fine.

It would be reasonable to expect that the intensity of the war in Europe and the atmosphere of national crisis might temper the enthusiasm of the Burston strikers and their supporters. On the contrary. The issue was kept very much alive throughout the four years of the war, and both sides constantly re-affirmed their determination to settle for nothing short of unconditional surrender. George Edwards and W. B. Taylor, the only Labour members on the County Council, fought a lonely and unsuccessful battle to have the inquiry re-opened. The Education Committee spent much of its time reading and acknowledging petitions from trades unions, political organizations and Labour and Trades Councils, all demanding the re-instatement of the Burston schoolteachers. For a short time, it was generally believed that the state of emergency and the serious shortage of qualified teachers might improve the Higdons' chances of regaining their jobs, at least for the duration of the war. But the Education Committee was not looking for an easy way out of its difficulties, and the idea was quickly scotched.

Finally, Arthur Henderson, the recently appointed President of the Board of Education, offered his services as an arbitrator. In a carefully worded letter he suggested 'that three members of the Education Committee should meet three persons representing Mr and Mrs Higdon to consider the Burston School difficulty, with a view to arriving at an agreement.' He added that he recognized he had no right to interfere officially, but was prepared to act in his personal capacity and would either attend the meeting or appoint a representative.

Mrs Higdon agreed to the proposal on two conditions. First,

the Education Committee had to promise that, if arbitration went in her favour, they would re-instate her in Burston School. The second condition was addressed to the National Union of Teachers, and required the Union to undertake a vigorous propaganda campaign on her behalf in the event of the Education Committee refusing arbitration. Neither the N.U.T. nor the Authority was prepared to give satisfactory assurances, and Arthur Henderson's offer was turned down.

But the Higdons were not at all perturbed by the failure of the preliminary negotiations. They were already at work on a plan which, if successful, promised a future more exciting than a schoolteacher's career in the employment of the Norfolk County Council. When the children were evicted from their classroom in the carpenter's shop, the Strike Committee was faced with the problem of finding alternative accommodation. Property was scarce, and, since there appeared to be no possibility of an early settlement of the dispute, they adopted the only possible course of action. A £5,000 appeal was launched for the purpose of building a Burston Strike School.

With George Lansbury as president of the fund-raising committee, the scheme gained immediate popularity with some trade unions and Labour associations, who recognized the immense potential of a school constructed with the sole aid of socialist funds and dedicated to socialist principles. If the Burston project was a success, who could deny that other areas might be capable of following the lead? Labour schools could be set up all over the country.

This latest development convinced a few members of the County Council that their Education Committee had grossly mishandled the case. Surely an entire village could not engage on such an act of defiance without just cause? The suggestion that the dismissal of Mrs Higdon was motivated by the political and social activity of her husband was firmly repudiated, but on the other hand the available evidence indicates that the recommendations of the tribunal were determined to some extent by the prejudice of the school managers.

In January 1917, George Edwards announced his intention of

reviving his campaign for a public inquiry. An appropriate motion was set down for the next meeting of the County Council. The Education Committee, hounded on all sides by hostile critics, appealed to Edwards to postpone the debate until each member had received a copy of a confidential report on the Higdons and their relations with their employers. Edwards agreed, and the report was circulated in time for a special meeting of the County Council at the end of that month.

A major section of the document was devoted to an account of the events which led to the crisis at Wood Dalling, where the Higdons had worked before their appointment at Burston. The Committee defended its position by arguing:

... Mrs Higdon's inability to work harmoniously with her Managers is at the root of the trouble. ... The Sub-Committee who held the first enquiry at Wood Dalling heard unmistakable evidence of the way in which the Head Teachers could act and address the Managers.

The fact that since Mrs Higdon left Wood Dalling there has been no friction between the Teaching Staff and the Managers and that at Burston, neither before the appointment of Mrs Higdon nor since her leaving, has there been any case of friction between the Teachers and their Managers, is indicative of the source of the trouble.

... The Burston decision is only the climax of a series of complaints involving two enquiries at Wood Dalling. ...

... It has been affirmed that during the last four years of his stay at Wood Dalling (1906–10) Mr Higdon's work for the Agricultural Labourers' Union in Wood Dalling and the surrounding villages, and his subsequent election to the Parish Council were the cause of friction with the Managers; but as early as 2 May 1904, the Clerk of the Wood Dalling Managers wrote to the Committee:

'Both Teachers ignore the Managers altogether and are scarcely on speaking terms, with one exception, which is the late Chairman. I think he is the only one they even acknowledge. There is a feeling that a change in both cases is desirable. ...'

Two years later, in 1906, the Committee dismissed one of the Managers for calling Mrs Higdon a liar at a meeting, when the Managers are stated to have been called 'humbugs' by the Head Teacher.

... The first enquiry at Wood Dalling was held on 1 December 1908. ... The Sub-Committee reported as follows:

'1. The friction between Mr and Mrs Higdon and the Managers is

89

so great that some of the Managers will not visit the school as they are afraid of the treatment they will receive.

'2. The Teachers attribute what they consider the enmity of the Managers towards them to the fact that they have charged some of the Managers with illegally employing children. . . .

'3. Mr Higdon charged the Chairman with using abusive language to him and the Chairman denied this and said it was Mr Higdon who abused him.

'4. The Managers said that the Teachers do not recognize them as Managers. . . . '

On 17 July 1910, a second enquiry was necessitated owing to further friction between the Managers and the Head Teacher. The Sub-Committee reported as follows . . . :

'That the state of friction between the Head Teacher and the Managers which existed when the former enquiry was held in December 1908, when the Teacher was brought before the Committee and admonished that she "must treat her Managers with courtesy and carry out their instructions if she was to remain in the service of the Committee", still existed, and that in consequence we find it undesirable for the Teacher to remain as Mistress of this school. . . .'

. . . on 2 August the Head Teacher was asked to send in her resignation as the least prejudicial form of removal from the school. . . . As on 17 October the resignation requested on 2 August had not been received, the Head Teacher was given three months' notice. . . . Mr Higdon, on 24 October, received a month's notice to terminate his engagement. . . . On 30 November, under pressure from outside, Mrs Higdon [expressed] 'sincere regret for my want of discretion in addressing some of the Managers of the Wood Dalling School in a discourteous manner'. . . . As a consequence of this letter . . . the Committee, on 17 December, offered to endeavour to transfer Mrs Higdon and her husband to Burston School. . . .

Some months afterwards, it was brought to the Committee's notice that Mrs Higdon, before leaving Wood Dalling School, made the entry in the log book respecting her case, which was of such a character that the Board of Education suggested it should be expunged.

At first glance, the evidence was weighted heavily against the Higdons. How was it possible to defend two irresponsible schoolteachers who, after jeopardizing their careers in one school, wantonly abused their second chance to make good? It is as well, however, to judge the accusations of the managers in both Wood Dalling and Burston in their proper perspective. While the Higdons were undoubtedly tactless and even ill-mannered in their relations with the education authorities, their employers were inclined to over-emphasize the need for obedience and respect. At the Burston inquiry for example, the Reverend Eland complained that on one occasion Mrs Higdon failed to acknowledge his daughter when they passed in the street. Her behaviour was crude, yet hardly the material for evidence in an appeal for disciplinary action. And, despite the protestations of the Education Committee, the political factor cannot be ignored. In both villages the Boards of Managers were dominated by anti-socialists who regarded the Higdons and the Agricultural Labourers' Union with fear and mistrust. At best, as George Edwards pointed out, the County Councillors who conducted the Burston inquiry 'allowed themselves to be biased by the political prejudice of one or two of the Managers'.

Finally, the bitterest opponents of the Higdons had to admit that, on occasion, their impatience and stubbornness were justified. The use of the open fireplace in Burston School was condemned by the managers as a needless extravagance even after the building was proved to be damp. Certainly, Mrs Higdon's knowledge of health education was far superior to that of her employers. Nor could it be denied that the schoolteachers invariably acted in the best interests of their pupils. Was it true that the Wood Dalling managers employed children illegally? The Education Committee declined to answer the question, and the Higdons must be allowed the benefit of the doubt.

But whatever arguments are raised in defence of this extraordinary couple, the fact remains that they were totally incapable of accepting advice or direction. Even their political allies recognized their tendency to abuse power. At a constituency Labour Party meeting held in 1919 to nominate a candidate for the South Norfolk by-election, Thomas Higdon was awarded one vote. His two opponents gained forty and sixteen votes respectively.

The County Councillors who attended the special meeting in late January 1917 accepted the conclusions of the confidential report. As far as the Education Committee was concerned, the Higdon file was closed, and even the subsequent investigation by the N.U.T., which drew attention to serious irregularities in the Burston inquiry, failed to influence their decision. A final statement, in the form of a Committee resolution, was published in February 1918:

Seeing that the Education Committee's decision was based on a full and impartial enquiry in February 1914 into all the circumstances of the case, at which enquiry the Teacher was defended by a Standing Counsel of the N.U.T.; that as evidenced by published statements, the Committee's decision was accepted by the Tenure Committee of the N.U.T., and its action endorsed by the Conference of the N.U.T in 1916; and further seeing that the County Council have adopted and subsequently endorsed the Committee's findings; and that nothing has arisen since the enquiry was held to lead the Committee to doubt the justice of their decision, this Committee, as the responsible Authority, declines to re-open the case.

The County Council made no attempt to hinder the work of the schoolteachers in Burston. The appeal for the Strike School fell short of its target, and raised only £1,000, but George Lansbury laid the foundation stone in May 1917, and building began on a site allocated by the Parish Council, which was still controlled by Higdon and his associates. The work was completed in early 1918, and already Mrs Higdon had quarrelled with the members of the Strike Committee. The treasurer had to report to the N.U.T. that the funds were exhausted, and there were liabilities of £150 owing to the builder. Not unnaturally, the executive were reluctant to involve themselves in the launching of a new system of public education, and strictly limited their commitment to the payment of a victimization salary. Mrs Higdon, meanwhile, had been asserting herself again, and had formed her own committee of local residents who gained control of the finances of the school.

When the Strike School opened, there were about forty children listed on the attendance register. They worked in a single, unpretentious classroom – with two fireplaces and a generous quota of windows! On the outside wall surrounding the front entrance, each brick was engraved with the name of a person or organization who contributed to the Strike School Fund.

The standard of education was no more than average for a village community, but the social ideals which the Higdons shared with the parents were handed on to the children, who developed a strong and lasting interest in political affairs. Thomas Higdon spent much of his time writing and played little part in the day-to-day business of teaching, but whenever he attended a union or party meeting he took with him a party of older pupils. Perhaps unconsciously he was carrying out the first successful experiments in applied civics for younger citizens.

The Higdons, settled in their own school, now basked in the national publicity which came their way, and made use of it to recruit students from all over the country. A widely circulated pamphlet, published in 1919, served the double purpose of appealing for additional funds for the school and advertising the benefits of a Burston education:

We thank you for the support we have received in aid of our fight, and for carrying on the work of the strike school. We are herewith sending you our statement of accounts, from which it will appear that funds are still needed, so that comrades and societies wishing to help need not hesitate to do so.

The school strike, which began on 1 April 1914, has now been in existence over five years, and has thus seen the war in and out; and still the parents, children, and teachers and their supporters in Burston are solidly united in their protest against injustice and tyranny and in their fight for Freedom.

Many of the scholars who first came out on strike, have, of course, left school and gone to work, but forty children are still attending the strike school, and such is the hold of this new democratic, educational and social movement upon the life of the village that most of the infants who come along find their way to the school and take the places of the older children who are constantly leaving. Thus what began as a strike of school-children on behalf of their teacher, and was spoken of by the rector, chairman of the school managers, as 'all moonshine', 'a nine-days wonder' etc., etc., has become a permanent Socialist Educational Cause and Institution [and] . . . 'The first Trades Union School in England'.

The day may come when the Labour movement will officially recognize and finance the strike school, but at present the school depends upon the voluntary contributions of individual sympathizers and the donations of T.U. branches and social societies as seen by the attached balance sheets. Our friends will do us a great service in helping to make our school known in this direction by handing on this circular to other branches or by sending us the names and addresses of Branch secretaries.

This voluntary support has the advantage of leaving the school free and unfettered by officialdom of any kind, provided it is not hampered by lack of funds. . . . The fight has ever been sustained, and the work of the school regularly turned out by the constant unity and devotion of the pupils and teachers.

Arrangements are made for boarding scholars, should comrades living at some distance desire to avail themselves of the opportunity of sending their children to the strike school. Burston is a very healthy village. Medical advice for the strike school costs nothing, it is so seldom required. Burston breezes, Burston bread (home-made) and the strike school buildings are all of the best, and it has been remarked that 'the children look the picture of health'. Their playground is the beautiful common, a heritage preserved for them by their forefathers, who fought and died for the common rights of Norfolk.

The new strike school building, besides serving as a free Elementary Day School and for the training of the children in the principles of freedom and socialism, is also used for public meetings on Sundays and week nights in connection with the strike, the Agricultural Labour Union and moral and revolutionary propaganda generally. It is the centre of a new, living movement of educational and social activity which together with the building itself and the many inscriptions on its walls will, it is hoped, form the best lasting memorial of the villagers' fight for Freedom and Justice.

It is from the wider national character of our fight, as well as from the local aspects of it, that we feel we can commend our Cause to all sections of the Labour movement.

In the 1920s, two members of a Russian trade delegation arranged to have their children educated in Burston. During the period of the General Strike, they were joined by youngsters from six mining families. One of the boys lived with the Higdons until 1938, when he enlisted in the navy. Granville Giles, a London teacher who was later to become the first, and only, Communist president of the N.U.T., sent his eldest son to the school for one year.

Thomas Higdon was defeated in the Parish Council elections of 1918, when the country was engulfed in a wave of conservatism, but a few months later he contributed to the election of George Edwards, the first Labour M.P. to represent a genuinely rural constituency. He remained treasurer of the National Union of Agricultural Workers throughout the inter-war years. His fiercest opponent, the Reverend Charles Eland, left Burston in 1920 and died two years later.

The Strike School prospered until the mid-1930s, when both teachers were well beyond retirement age. Mrs Higdon characteristically ignored the advice of her friends, and refused to employ an assistant. By 1939 – the year Thomas Higdon died – there were only a handful of pupils left. The younger parents could not remember the days of the strike; some of them had not even been born when the Higdons and their children declared independence. They could not have the same resentment against the council and school managers as the older people in the village. In any case, the state system of school administration had mellowed with the years. Teachers were treated with greater respect and consideration by their employers and though managers still, in theory, possessed considerable powers (they could, for instance, veto the appointment of a head teacher) social relations had progressed to a point where discussion and compromise were generally preferred to a head-on clash. Even so there were, and still are, plenty of opportunities for a governing body to make life intolerable for a head teacher.

At Burston there seemed little chance that managers or local education authority would risk another major confrontation. The Strike School was no longer needed and Mrs Higdon, who continued working for a few months after her husband's death, was clearly incapable of carrying out her normal duties. She was found wandering in her garden at night and, on one occasion, met Violet Potter, then a grown woman and no longer a young strike leader, and asked her politely : 'Are you coming to school, Violet?'

Mrs Higdon survived the Second World War, when her school was used as a furniture store, and died in 1947. The National Union of Agricultural Workers set up a representative committee of trustees, and the following year the building took on a new lease of life when it was opened as a village hall and a social centre.

About this time Tom Potter, an ex-pupil of Burston Strike School, stood as a Communist candidate in the Parish Council elections. It would have pleased the Higdons to know that the principles on which they based their teaching were remembered in the village in which they fought and were buried. When the results were declared, Tom Potter was top of the poll.

1. The Malting House, Cambridge, where Pyke lived and started his school. It is virtually unchanged today. This picture, and those that follow, were originally stills from a film taken of the school but destroyed in the war. They represent the only pictorial record that remains.

2. An open-air lunch session at the Malting House School. In the middle of the picture is Susan Isaacs, the director of the project. The other teacher is Dr Evelyn Lawrence.

3. Small children at work in the science laboratory of the Malting House School. The boy is using a Bunsen burner in his experiment.

4. The Malting House workshop. This picture shows dramatically the policy of the school to let children use real tools and not scaled-down, toy versions.

5. The children at the Malting House chose their own records, and operated the gramophone themselves. At other times, Susan Isaacs played to them on the piano, or taught them songs.

6. A discussion with Susan Isaacs outside the tent pitched in the gardens of the Malting House. Some children have taken their shoes off, others have kept them on. There were few rules.

7. A detail from a group photograph, showing the Higdons outside the Strike School at Burston.

8. The Strike School children, posing on the village green. Burston Church, the centre of opposition to the whole movement, is in the background.

9. Burston Strike School soon after completion. The doors and windows are wide open, a strict rule imposed by Mrs Higdon, a great believer in invigorating ventilation even in cold weather.

10. Bricks paid for by organizations and individuals sympathetic to the strike cause cover much of the front of Burston Strike School. The foundation stone stands as a perpetual memorial to the class war.

11. Three eleven-year-old boys at work on the now famous, but obliterated, murals at Ivy Lane School, Chippenham. This panel, 'Summer', was carried out without any disruption of the rest of the class.

12. Another boy at work on a second panel, 'Autumn'. These murals, painted in the early thirties, are referred to in the Plowden Report on primary schools as an example of the artistic capabilities of young children.

13. 'The Making of the Golden Calf', painted in water colours in 1930 by a ten-year-old Wiltshire boy. A typical example of the strong sense of design that marked the work of some of these children.

14. 'Christmas : The Angels and the
Shepherds', a 12 × 12 ins. linoleum
cut by a twelve-year-old at Ivy Lane
School. This was only one of the
many media used by the children.

15. The School Council in session at Forest School. Everyone, no matter what their age or position, had one vote and complete freedom of speech.

16. The children at Forest School learned music not merely by playing, but by making the instruments, such as pipes, drums and tambourines, themselves.

17. Forest School children made their own toys. However young, they were encouraged to fend for themselves. This boy probably brought the wood from the forest and planed and shaped it himself.

18. Camping was a natural part of the school's activities. Today, the Forest School camps for young children remain to form an unbroken link with the ideals of the original experiment in the New Forest.

19. A picture of Henry Morris taken at Cambridge shortly before he retired as Chief Education Officer for the county.

20. Impington Village College, Cambridge, opened in 1938. The classrooms, with their sliding doors leading into the college grounds, embody Morris's idea of flexibility and the use of space in the learning environment.

Art and Craft: Marion Richardson and Robin Tanner

*The moment was certainly ripe for those teachers, scattered
throughout England in towns and villages, who believed in Art
and Craft as the birthright of every boy and girl, to go ahead, and
this they did. Many encountered opposition and prejudice, and
there was for a while great difficulty in finding suitable materials
with which to work. Yet that great educational advance of
which they were a part is now generally recognized as one of the
major revolutions of this century in the teaching of young children.*
Primary Education, H.M.S.O., 1959 (p. 216)

In 1927, when unemployment and inflation were spreading like
cancer through Europe, one small event took place which,
though it was not planned that way, nevertheless proved to be
a significant milestone in the history of education in Britain. It
was an art exhibition.

It was held in London and sponsored by the Save the Children Fund. The Fund had arranged for a collection of children's paintings to be brought over from Vienna, where they
had been produced under the tutelage of Franz Cizek by a group
of gifted children. As early as 1898 Professor Cizek had opened
free classes for children of school age in the School of Applied
Art in Vienna, where he worked. Twice a week, for years,
learners came to these sessions to draw and paint as the mood
took them. Their works were, indeed, remarkable. In the first
place they were large, when it was generally thought that children could use only small areas of paper. Secondly, they were
incredibly detailed and stylized. They were full of vigour and
colour, when children's art was commonly held to be dull and
derivative. They were also rather sentimental, depicting flowers,
animals and little girls posing like graceful ornaments at one
with nature. They sparked off an immediate popular appeal.
Two of them were bought by Christian Schiller, later to become
a staff Inspector at the Ministry of Education.

'I was inspired. ... We hung the paintings in our nursery, and
our own children grew up with them. Although Cizek moulded

97

the work of his pupils into a single distinctive style which we would now regard as sentimental and stilted, these paintings were revolutionary to people like myself, for they showed what could be done, what children could achieve if only . . .'

Years afterwards, Schiller recalled that 'it was as if the convictions we had always had of the potential of young people was suddenly presented, alive, before us. You must remember that the concept that each child was different and unique, and that each was capable of making an individual contribution and a personal statement was not merely not established; it was simply not accepted by the majority. Throughout the country there was a sort of "underground" of teachers who, convinced that this was the case, were working towards a single goal, not only through art and craft, but in every sphere of education.'

The Cizek exhibition provided a focal point for this 'underground'. It was the first public statement of a philosophy which they had been fostering for many years and which they would have to continue to force upon the public conscience. With Cizek, these men and women were suddenly given a sign not merely that they were on the right lines, but that, ultimately, their views would triumph. 'That great educational advance of which they were a part is now generally recognized as one of the major revolutions of this century in the teaching of young children,' was the official verdict in 1959.

One of those who went to the London exhibition was Marion Richardson, who said afterwards that 'they aroused the very deepest interest and were a revelation to most people. Their size and their brilliance astonished every one; so did the sense of decoration and the assurance with which they had been painted.' Marion Richardson, born and reared in the Midlands, had had, in the early years of the century, a very different art education. She had been forced to struggle with inanimate objects that alone were considered suitable subjects for drawing. 'I was only sixteen when I went to the Birmingham School of Art to sit for the entrance examination which decided all awards. How well I remember the crab's claw which was part of our test! As I drew it the horrid thing seemed to be clutching me, and, though feeling obliged to do my very best, I hoped with all my heart that this best would not be good enough to win a scholar's place. I did not want to leave school, and had no interest in learning to draw. But, alas, the crab had caught me. The offer of four years' training as a teacher could not be refused, and that autumn I became an art student.'

During her stay at art school, Marion Richardson followed the set curriculum: more crabs' claws, bathroom taps, umbrellas, ivy leaves and an unrelenting dose of plaster casts from classical sculpture were placed before her to draw in meticulous line as a training for the day when she would be expected to move into the schools and repeat the exercise with her young pupils. Although she rebelled inwardly at this stilted interpretation of art, her natural ability won through and before the end of her stay, at the age of nineteen, she was appointed art mistress at Dudley Girls' High School. She wore a veil at the interview in an attempt to look older. 'Young as I was, I was eager to hand on as well as I possibly could the teaching I now possessed.'

Dudley is an extension of Birmingham: an urban appendix of shops, houses and light engineering works sprawling outwards into the Warwickshire countryside. 'No one, I think, could ever regard Dudley as a beautiful place, and yet its strange ups and downs, its sudden lights and sunken pools, stirred me as nothing had before; and once I began to use the local scene, given in the form of a word picture, my problem was not to find, but to choose from a wealth of subjects that flooded my mind. Everywhere I looked the scene fell into a picture – fell into a kind of harmony, a music of shapes. I used to ask the children what it was that made a picture. "When everything rhymes," someone said.'

In her first year at Dudley as art mistress, Marion Richardson began to evolve her ideas about the role of art in education, about how to teach it and how to inspire her children. She was influenced, during her first summer at the school before the First World War, by an exhibition at the Grafton Galleries in

London of a collection of Post-Impressionist paintings. As she looked at these works, she imagined she saw her children at work. 'It was an odd experience, and one that is almost impossible to put into words. In the happiest of the children's work I had learned to recognize a vital something; but with only my limited knowledge of art I had not, up till then, been fully conscious of having seen it elsewhere. Now, for the first time, it blazed at me; and it seemed that I need never again mistake the sham for the real in art.'

Her pupils were, each morning, given piles of paper on which to work out their imaginings. They used water colours, but were allowed complete freedom in the way they applied their palettes. They were taken on outings to art galleries. Above all, their teacher told them stories and 'word pictures' in which the children sat on the floor around her with their eyes shut while she read either a poem to evoke some particular scene, like Masefield's 'Twilight' ('Twilight it is, and the far woods are dim, and the rooks cry and call. Down in the valley the lamps, and the mist, and a star over all ...') or a prose description of something that had caught the discerning Richardson eye in the environs of Dudley.

All this was in direct contrast to accepted methods and standards of art teaching, and, moreover, in opposition to the examinations set for the School Certificate, which demanded academic proficiency in the drawing of models, to be marked and scored by the teacher. A way had to be found in her own new methods for coping with such external pressures.

'How it was I am not quite sure, but in the half-dark room I happened upon the idea of lighting a group of models by an electric bicycle lamp. This cast long shadows which linked the objects and gave the group a most moving and dramatic quality. One of the girls said, when she saw it, that it looked like a little stage. This gave my mind a jolt. The bicycle lamp had lifted the objects out of the light of common day into a dream world of wonder and delight ... for my next lesson I whitewashed a set of ninepins ... another model that we all enjoyed was five big basins set about on a sheet or mirror ...'

Then she began to improvise the materials. The size of the paper which was laid down by the authorities was doubled. Sugar paper, with its coarse, soft texture, and cartridge paper were brought into the classroom. The children were given charcoal, conte crayons, soft pencils, powder and poster paints, eventually tempera and gouache, coloured waterproof and Indian inks, dyes and stains, pens and stiles, brushes of hog bristle or sable, tubes of oils and real palettes.

Marion Richardson also came to feel that she now needed the stimulus of London for her teaching, and applied for a post in the city. But at the interview, she was made aware that her pioneering work was indeed just that; that outside the cloisters of Dudley Girls' High School, the world of education stood unbelieving and unchanged.

'With tremendous care I chose the examples of children's work that the Selection Committee had asked to see and, although I hardly expected to succeed myself, I did not dream that the very best of our precious work would meet with disapproval. Alas, it did. I shall never forget how the same little picture that had been so full of meaning and interest for me seemed merely incompetent and crude when passed from one member to another of that alarming Committee. I wanted to run away and hide. Were my standards all wrong? Was I failing in my duty to the Dudley children?'

This kind of pervading doubt, the feeling of operating in a vacuum with, outside, a hostile, sceptical world, affected every one of the early pioneers in art education. What they sought was a dialogue of acceptable criticism and sympathetic understanding. What they got was ridicule. Yet towards the end of the First World War, Marion Richardson had already progressed to a point where her children had linked up with representatives of the Manchester cotton trade, whose factories used the block-printed designs worked out at Dudley for materials sold around the world, and her work was well enough known for her to get an invitation to join the London Day Training College, headed by Professor Percy Nunn, as a tutor in the college's new graduate course for art students.

Art and Craft: Marion Richardson and Robin Tanner

One of her exercises with students was to ask them to compete against her Dudley children, whom she continued to see two days a week, in a colour training game. At each end of a room, from a beam running along the ceiling, hung skeins of wool of differing shades : white and near white, yellow, orange, red and pink, blue, green, violet and purple, buff and brown, grey and black, mottled and marled. On one side of the room the skeins were permanently fixed and numbered, on the other side their matching threads were detachable, hanging over hooks. The children were given certain numbers, asked to look at the corresponding colour of wool, and then run across the room and choose the matching shade. One small child, still unable to read, would select the right shade nineteen times in a row. The college staff never once defeated a team of chidren at the game.

Now this same kind of work was carried further, to Benenden girls' school in Kent, and among the many parties of children who came to the college. Gradually, the idea that art education was not merely possible, but positively beneficial to children was being spread. And then came the Cizek exhibition and the public revelation that the art of the child was a natural and creative passion, to be fostered and enjoyed as any other creative expression.

Marion Richardson, who went on to become an L.C.C. inspector and develop the writing patterns for which she is now chiefly remembered, continued to train a succession of teachers and to influence the course of art education. In 1967, John Blackie, who himself retired as Chief H.M.I. of Primary Education, said of her :

When she began her work in London in 1930 art in elementary schools was unspeakably dull. It consisted mainly of drawing models with an HB pencil. Such colour as was used was watercolour (a notoriously difficult and subtle medium to handle), and this was applied to drawings of plants. Drawing paper was used, and, since this was very expensive and requisition funds were limited, it was cut into small rectangles 8 ins. × 5 ins. or even less. Very few children were capable of using these materials and limitations creatively.

Art and Craft: Marion Richardson and Robin Tanner

Marion Richardson encouraged the use of large sheets of cheap paper – sometimes even old newspapers were used – of large brushes which would hold plenty of colour, of powder paints which were. cheap to use and could produce solid masses of colour, and she suggested that the children should be allowed to paint what they liked and not be given subjects or models. The results of this, as it then seemed, wildly revolutionary policy was that young children began to produce paintings which many adult art critics found very exciting. They typically set about painting a picture without a moment's pause, with extraordinary confidence and apparently with a clear purpose in their minds. Anyone who has watched infants painting must have noticed this. . . .*

*

One man who noticed it was Robin Tanner. He was born in Bristol in 1904 ('On a Sunday, so you can see, I was destined to be a nuisance'), the third of six children in a quite poor family in which the mother, an imaginative woman and a pacifist, was the driving force and the father, a worker in wood, the craftsman. From the first, Robin's career seemed destined. As a child of seven, he used to escort his friends to a field, spanned by a sheltering railway arch near his home. Here he would present each of them with paper and crayons and stern instructions to draw something, with prizes of shaped pebbles or skeleton leaves he had collected, or tiny patterns of petals and grasses arranged inside the lids of tins.

Robin Tanner knew he was meant to be an artist, but he also wanted to teach. This was the era of the student-teacher, and on leaving school he spent a year teaching at Chippenham in Wiltshire. On four days each week, there was his work with children; on the fifth, all the student-teachers of Wiltshire – about twelve of them – met at a centre in Trowbridge to continue their own education. The teacher was Agnes Grist, 'Mistress of Method' at Salisbury Training College and a woman who exercised a deep influence on her pupils. She was supposed to provide a sort of potted training course, but instead gave them lessons in logic, architecture, botany, the administration

* *Inside the Primary School* (H.M.S.O. 1967), pp. 112–13.

of justice and English. To those in her class it seemed a perfectly reasonable choice of subjects.

It was at Goldsmiths' College in London that Robin Tanner first trained for teaching. From there he took a job at Black-heath Road Boys' School in Greenwich, and when the day was over walked to Goldsmiths' College of Art to study, until nine-thirty in the evenings, drawing and etching. It took him three-and-a-half years to save enough money from his work to devote his full time to studying art and later to practise as a profes-sional print-maker.

'I never knew ugliness until I came to south-east London : then I saw enough to fill my life many times over,' he recalled later. There were sixty-one in his class at Blackheath Road at first, the children sitting in galleries among walls of shiny privet green and cow colour : infants on the ground floor, girls on the first, boys on the second. Nearly all the children came from ex-tremely mean streets around Deptford Broadway and from the bottom of the hill leading to the heath. About a third were Jewish. Walking from his Old Dover Road rooms across Black-heath to school in the early morning, he saw not only the squalor of the children's lives, but also the devotion which many of their families – particularly the Jewish ones – ex-pended on them, at a time when unemployment was rife and money was impossibly scarce.

The hardship of those days, as they were reflected in the children, is difficult to describe. Christian Schiller, who was at the London Day Training College a year or two before Marion Richardson, saw it from the slums of Liverpool, where he was sent as a young Ministry Inspector. 'It was just before the General Strike, and the life of the city shocked me. I got a single room somewhere near the docks and began work with a kind of missionary zeal. What I found was horrifying. At one school there were eighty-six children in a single class, fully a third sitting in a coal-hole. Families of six or more children lived in a single room. Schools consisted of long halls in which perhaps five classes, each one of them with more than fifty children in them, occupied the same four walls, so that the accent was on strict conformity, silence and absolute obedience if chaos was to be kept to a minimum.

'I remember one child in particular. The five-year-olds always sat in "galleries", rows of them tiered upwards. It was always very difficult to get these wan children, some of them so thin and many of them sewn up in their clothes for the winter, saturated in eucalyptus oil to hide the smell of their bodies, to make any kind of response to questions. As I was going round I saw a little girl who was getting all her sums wrong. I went to talk to her and she shrank back, as if I was going to hit her. But I went and sat next to her, and gradually she began to talk to me. It turned out that, being the eldest in a family that had two other daughters and a baby brother, it was her job to buy the breakfast in the morning before coming to school – there was not enough money to buy provisions for more than a day ahead. With a silver sixpence she had provided for the entire family, getting the traditional "screw" of tea, the porridge, sugar and all the other things, eking out each penny. And then she came to school and got her sums wrong! The poor thing was almost starved, and white with lack of sleep.'

It was to this kind of setting that Robin Tanner, apprentice etcher and inexperienced teacher, came. It was his task at Greenwich to teach his pupils everything – how to write, how to read, how to draw, how to think. He seized the opportunity as if it were the road to a fortune. He took them out of the school to the Tate Gallery, an unheard-of innovation. He used whitewash on the huge sheets of oaty brown paper in which the school supplies were packed, and let the children paint on this, at first with the garish distemper colours sold by ironmongers. But a stock cupboard yielded up a long-forgotten store of pastels, and he and his pupils ground these down to powder with pestle and mortar, mixed it with weak size and produced their own serviceable body colour, which the boys used freely.

One afternoon, on a walk back to school after an outing to the Thames to look at the tugs the boys had been painting in their pictures, one group suggested a bathe in the river. They knew it would not be allowed. 'You could easily *imagine* you

were paddling and swimming in the Thames. What about painting a picture of it tomorrow?' asked Robin Tanner. And they
did. A group worked at a mural in an unused room at the very
top of the building. Their spirited design of naked boys splash-
ing about in the water delighted H. W. Nunn, the sympathetic
headmaster, but a young L.C.C. inspector was full of shocked
disapproval. 'Anyhow, the painting only shows that young children can't draw properly, doesn't it?' he said. 'You see, they
aren't ready for the human figure yet.'

Christian Schiller was meeting the same kind of frustrations
in Liverpool. 'What was so terrible, apart from the crowding
and the conditions, was the regimentation. We longed to let the
children grow, to give them their heads. I remember one infant school in my area where I found six children, lying full
length on the floor, working with hog's hair brushes and jam
jars of paint on huge sheets of newspaper, an unheard-of freedom which we tried to encourage all the time. Other teachers
sat up throughout the night whitewashing newspapers so that
their children, who were only provided with small slips of
regulation-sized paper, could have enough space to paint in the
morning. Imagine it – whitewashing newspaper in the night for
use the next day! But most education authorities held that this
was a pointless effort, that it was a question of "second denti-
tion". The children had to have their second set of teeth before
they were ready to tackle anything of either a creative or an
intellectual capacity.'

Robin Tanner, working in London, became more and more
convinced of the power of child art. Later he was to record this
belief that a child

is in some respects a singularly complete artist. He knows exactly
what he likes and what he wants, and he is ready to try his best
to produce this. ... Children are daring, and approach their work in
a spirit of adventure, so that it is fresh and individual; they do not
try to strain the medium with which they are working, and in my
experience they have very great patience, and can easily be trained
to a sense of craftsmanship.*

Children's Work in Block Printing (Dryad Press, Leicester, 1936), p. 8.

It was this conviction which he brought to his second school, Ivy Lane, at Chippenham – where he had begun as a student-teacher. He had left London for his beloved north-west Wiltshire – always to be the source of inspiration for his own etchings – not to resume teaching but to continue his art work. But the headmaster of the local school, F. H. Hinton (father of Lord Hinton, the atomic scientist), persuaded him to return to the classroom. Hinton was a remarkable man. He had an undeserved reputation as a martinet, but his ideas on education were far ahead of his time and he was anxious to give the young London schoolmaster-etcher every chance to bring his own ideas into the school. Ivy Lane at this time – the late twenties and early thirties – was a typical all-age school for boys and girls from three to fourteen, the sons and daughters of workers in both agriculture and industry. It was here that Robin Tanner came of age as a teacher.

He taught not only art and craft but English, arithmetic, Scripture and what was known as P.T. Once a week he taught English ecclesiastical architecture to a keen W.E.A. class in Swindon, a class made up of railway workers. On Saturdays, he travelled to various centres throughout the country, talking about painting, and teaching design and crafts to other teachers. The children at Ivy Lane were encouraged to make their own notebooks in place of those supplied in bulk to the school, and the whole art of book production – involving handwriting, formal lettering, block printing, pattern designing and binding – became firmly established. Linoleum cutting was carried out on a large scale, and one group of teenagers etched on copper, pulling their proofs on their teacher's press at Kington Langley, the village outside Chippenham where Robin Tanner had made his home. In the crowded classrooms of Ivy Lane, substantial lengths of cotton and linen were printed from linoleum blocks – there was no art room – while other children might be printing a bedspread or a set of curtains and a further group were binding books. For drawing, every available kind of pencil, crayon and pen were used, and for painting, water colours, powder colours, inks and household oil-bound paints in large cans were brought in. The children were always asked to choose their own subjects, the majority of them inspired by the everyday life of the market town, by the surrounding countryside and by the Bible, especially the stories of the Apocrypha – of Tobit, Judith and Susanna – and the Song of the Holy Children.

If art is to be a living attitude of mind, then art teaching must encourage children to develop this attitude by expecting them to think and act for themselves, to perform personal pieces of work conceived and executed by them from start to finish, and therefore calling upon their own interests and resources, he believed. Children love making books, pictures and patterns, and are capable of far more sustained effort than many adults are aware. Too often they are not given enough to work on, or the work they are called upon to do is desultory.*

Turning his belief into action, Robin Tanner set the children to work to paint the school itself. One of the first to see the result was John Blackie. 'I was a very young inspector in September, 1932, and a few months afterwards – it was early in December, I think – my senior colleague, George Sutherland, took me to see Ivy Lane School. "I think you ought to see what's going on there," he told me, even though it was not in my area, so I had a look at this all-age elementary school, a very ordinary, solid, set kind of school. But what I remember is that Robin's classroom had four murals of the seasons on the walls: they weren't complete murals, but rather large pictures, and as far as I recall they had been executed directly on to the plaster. My immediate impression was that the children had seen rather a lot of Stanley and Gilbert Spencer and Paul Nash, they had that sort of quality. I remember saying to Robin Tanner: "You must have shown your children a lot of famous paintings."

' "Oh, no," he replied, "No, I don't show them anybody else's work. No, this is just them." I was staggered.'

One of the features common to the work of Robin Tanner at Ivy Lane and Marion Richardson at Dudley was their concept

* *Lettering for Children* (Dryad Press, Leicester, 1936), p. 32.

of art, which quickly spread from a concern with the acceptable
school activities of painting and drawing to encompass the
whole sweep of creative work. Robin Tanner let children cut
blocks and print with them at an early stage. He has maintained
a lifelong interest in calligraphy, and has always insisted that
handwriting is as much an expression of the artist as any other
form of personal expression. 'Of course,' he used to say, 'there's
nothing *wrong* with a pen, but what we give to our poor young
children is just *evil little spikes.*' What he wanted was stiff,
square-edged nibs, and good black ink : they were difficult to
find.

There is no child who does not like to use his hands and a few
tools, and if the art work of a school is bound up with doing sound,
everyday jobs, in the most fitting and seemly way possible – demanding imagination, intelligence and manual skill appropriate to
the age of the children – every child produces interesting work. Art
should be an attitude of mind to all work, and should not be regarded as a frill or something divorced from ordinary intelligence.
It should be bound up with everything we do, regarded neither as
mere licence nor as a set of purposeless exercises to be worked in
an unnatural or cramped way.*

This all-embracing attitude to art teaching was enriched by
his close friendship with a number of eminent artists. Marion
Richardson, in her own work, had won the support of the Fry
family and the Whitworth Art Gallery in Manchester, which
displayed her children's paintings and designs and led these to
be taken up by local industry. Robin Tanner remained, throughout his working life, an etcher of repute who as early as 1928
had his own work hanging in the Royal Academy exhibition
and six years later became an A.R.A. (It is an interesting footnote to his artistic career that when, in 1966, the Department
of Western Art at the Ashmolean Museum, Oxford, mounted an
exhibition of etchings and drawings by the artist F. L. Griggs,
the four artists included as Griggs's contemporaries were S. R.
Badmin, Paul Drury, Graham Sutherland and Robin Tanner, the
last three having been students together at Goldsmiths'.)

* *Children's Work in Block Printing,* p. 10.

Art and Craft: Marion Richardson and Robin Tanner

Robin Tanner's work as an artist and craftsman and his special interest in block-printed textiles created a bond between himself and Phyllis Barron who, with Dorothy Larcher, produced magnificent printed materials at Painswick in Gloucestershire. Inspired by their work, he resolved to continue his own art. 'If you cease to practise an art you can no longer teach it,' he would say. So he and his wife Heather set themselves the task of chronicling the life of the countryside at that time, she writing about the wild flowers, the people, the architecture of farms and cottages and the already disappearing crafts, while he made many etchings and drawings. The work took years to complete, but was eventually published by Collins as *Wiltshire Village*. It was published on the eve of war. During a blitz on Glasgow, the blocks for the illustrations were destroyed.

Robin Tanner's work never clashed with his teaching. He always insisted that children were natural artists and was emphatic that at Ivy Lane, formal though the conduct of the school appeared, nothing came in the way of setting the children free to flourish as both artists and craftsmen. Neither did anyone ever impose an authoritarian hand against him. In a story he tells against himself it was only his own 'teachery fear' that ever got in the way.

'I had brought the children to a point where they would stop at nothing; they were so confident and competent that problems of scale and of handling paint on wall surfaces did not daunt them, and they had an insatiable appetite for what they called "real jobs" – ambitious enterprises demanding sustained concentration.

'It was a boy whose father was a foreman of some sort on the Great Western Railway at Chippenham who first came to me, with several others, to tell me that he had told his father he considered the dismal brown waiting room on the "down" platform was a disgrace and had "arranged" with him that we should tackle it! There were to be four murals – one over the fireplace and one on each of the other walls. Moreover, the sizes had already been estimated and preliminary cartoons had been drawn; there was to be a children's excursion train to Weston-super-Mare, children swimming in the Avon at Chippenham, the river in flood at the Town Bridge and the annual Chippenham Flower Show.

'Realizing that I should let myself in for a host of administrative difficulties if I let the venture happen, I put all sorts of obstacles in the way. Where should we store materials? Where should we be able to borrow ladders? What about the public while the work was in progress? Supposing there was an accident? And so on. To this day I remember the look of dismay on those boys' faces at my lack of trust and my teachery fears. And I remember – and reproach myself – their entirely satisfactory answers to all my questions and doubts. I said I must consult the headmaster and the railway officials; I postponed reaching a decision.

'Fortunately, those children were so immersed in other enterprises that they were able, I think, to forgive my lack of courage, but my crime against them is always very present whenever I now use that drab waiting room. But for my holding back, that room would have been throbbing with the vitality and skill of those children. Except that brown has given place to grey, it is just as it was in 1929.'

The story is typical of Robin Tanner, in that he believed so acutely in the artistic qualities of childhood that a single barrier, one solitary incident in which conventional wisdom prevailed, has remained with him as a wound to his conscience.

'Robin was essentially concerned to take children back to natural objects, phenomena and materials as a source of inspiration, to get them looking carefully, comparing and discussing and then interpreting their impressions in different materials; he was not concerned with reproducing but with this personal interpretation, personal expression,' said a teacher who had been on his courses. 'This was not "art and craft" but "art and craft in education", and it was concerned with thought and the release of intelligence, with Piagetian concept formation, and it led directly to the use of language, both spoken and written. Art and craft meant going back to the natural world, observing, discussing, using books to deepen one's knowledge and extend one's impressions, and the expression of this graphically or in collections or arrangements and also in words. Handwriting was an aspect of this – thoughts ordered through observation, drawing, painting and making, and clarified by talking were then put down in as clear and beautiful a form as possible. Robin always seemed to imply that the ability to set down well on paper affected the quality, the orderliness of the statement.'

It is here that one sees the differences between these two great art teachers, Marion Richardson and Robin Tanner. Richardson was all feeling: life was a picture, to be set down with urgency and brilliance while the passion was hot on the palette. 'When a teacher frees the artist's vision within a child, he inspires him to find a completely truthful expression for it. The vision itself is so lovable that nothing short of sincerity will serve,' she wrote. Robin Tanner, a Quaker, saw art as a celebration of the universal discipline. The word, the carving, the etching, the shape of a steeple against the skyline, the inevitability of the seasons and their corresponding changes: all these were expressions of the one unity of being.

One can see this in his thoughts on pattern.

Everyone has a natural sense of pattern, which is displayed from infancy to old age, and is maintained in some degree even when it never received training or encouragement. A child enjoys repetition, whether visual or oral, of shapes or of sounds; he takes delight in arranging his bricks in lines or groups, and feels the pattern even of his arithmetical tables. He runs along a pavement, stepping once in each square and never on the lines, and plays the pattern game of running along the kerb two steps on and one step off. ... We feel the satisfaction of planting a garden, laying a meal, arranging our tools, all in a patterned way. Bricks in a wall, panes of glass in a window, boards in a floor, are all arranged in formal order, the method of construction producing the pattern. There are thousands of such repeating patterns in the things of our everyday lives, and most of them came about inevitably, and we never question them. We make patterns unconsciously many times a day through this sense of design, and it would seem natural, therefore, to use it for our own and common enjoyment.*

* *Children's Work in Block Printing*, p. 8.

Art and Craft: Marion Richardson and Robin Tanner

There are two key words in that passage – 'design' and 'enjoyment'. For Robin Tanner believed as much that life was to be enjoyed and sought after and explored as that the exploration was itself worth while, that there was something always to find, and that it led to a depth of understanding that unfolded the many turns of nature.

In September 1935 he was invited to London from his school in Chippenham and asked to join His Majesty's Inspectorate at the Board of Education. When he agreed to be elevated to this post, he joined a very young band of men and women who had been brought in on a wave of recruitment in the thirties to fill the gaps that would normally have been occupied by the men who fell in the First World War. The Inspectorate, which would at that time have been peopled by more senior staff, found itself with an infusion of Young Turks. There was Percy Wilson, an inspector at thirty-four and later to retire as the Senior Inspector at the Department of Education; George Allen, who joined at the age of thirty-eight; Martin Roseveare, who was only thirty when he went to the Board, and was later knighted; John Blackie, who came in at twenty-nine and retired as Chief Inspector of Primary Schools. It was this young band, inspired by the Hadow Reports of 1926 and 1931 on the adolescent and the primary schools, that Robin Tanner joined. The Hadow Report on the primary schools, one of the key educational documents of this century, had opened a door to the world of art. 'Hitherto the general tendency has been to take for granted the existence of certain traditional "subjects" and to present them to the pupils as lessons to be mastered,' it reported. 'There is a place for that method, but it is neither the only method, nor the method most likely to be fruitful between the ages of seven and eleven. What is required at least so far as much of the curriculum is concerned is to substitute for it methods which take as the starting point of the work of the primary school the experience, the curiosity and the awakening powers and interests of the children themselves ...'

Robin Tanner's first job as an H.M.I. was to go up to Leeds for two years, and it was while he was there that he met again the kind of disbelieving reaction against child art that dogged the whole field of education. At a meeting of teachers in a lecture theatre at Sheffield University, he produced some of the work of Ivy Lane. He brought all the paintings, printed textiles and books to the hall and created one of his now famous exhibitions, but when he rose to speak about the work he was hooted down by teachers who refused to believe that this was the product of children.

No matter how he protested, his audience would not accept that this was unaided work, insisting that he had done the painting and cut the linoleum blocks himself! He felt suddenly homesick for those West Country children whose spirit and talent he felt were being insulted. 'Well, one day you'll learn!' he told them. And many did.

There were also some inspired women teachers in the infant schools of Leeds, and they, more than any others, encouraged Robin Tanner to continue his work in the area. But from Leeds he was moved to Gloucestershire, where schools rigorously followed the programmes laid down by the Parents' National Educational Union, regularly sending their children's examination papers to be marked at the headquarters of the P.N.E.U. at Ambleside. In this educational straitjacket there was only meagre scope for broadening class activities. But these were difficult years everywhere. The elementary schools were still the waifs of the educational system, and despite the enlightenment breathed into them by individual teachers, inspectors and the authors of the 1931 Hadow Report, their development remained stunted in the shadows of financial crises and the prospects of war.

Throughout that war, Robin Tanner – who registered as a conscientious objector – worked less in Gloucestershire than in the city of Bristol, as one of a small team of Ministry inspectors. The very fact of war, with its destruction, shortages and frustrations, turned teachers towards the arts. In Bristol, as earlier at Leeds, it was particularly in the infant schools that the

humanizing influence of working with the hands, with whatever materials were available, was most deeply understood and
felt.

The war over, a new period of intense activity opened up.
Not only had the new Education Act of 1944 removed 'standard'
schools and made primary education more flexible, so that art
and craft had a real chance to live within these newly struc-
tured schools, but the surge of idealism that was evoked by the
experience of war produced a new drive for better conditions.
In Oxfordshire, where Robin Tanner was to work from 1956,
the Chief Education Officer, Allen Chorlton, had the idea of
appointing a County Adviser for the 178 scattered primary
schools throughout the county. What was wanted was someone
who would be 'the eyes and ears of the Committee', as the
advertisement put it, and would provide a link between the
many small village schools that made up the county system.
The person who successfully replied to that advertisement was
a young college lecturer, Edith Moorhouse, who had been the
head of an all-age school in Hertfordshire before coming on the
staff of the emergency teacher training college at Wall Hall near
Watford. To get the post, Edith Moorhouse took driving lessons,
put down £194 on a 1934 Austin 10 and set off for the wilds of
Oxfordshire.

Of all the 178 schools she had to visit, about 100 contained
only one, or at most, two teachers. They were all-age, rural
schools which were not merely small but incredibly isolated.
Six or seven children sat in a single, cast-iron desk, water was
brought from a village pump and the headmistress was often the
ageing, lonely figure of the spinster who had begun her career as
a pupil-teacher. There was one school where the head, a woman
of eighty-four, had attended her own school as a child, become a
pupil-teacher, stayed to become head and remained there at this
same school all her adult life. In these barn-walled, church-like
buildings, where staff rooms were unknown and the *per capita*
allowance per child on books of all kinds was 5s. 6d. a year,
where the activities of the next village a mile away were a
matter of hearsay and Oxford was Babylon, new approaches to

the teaching of any subject might have been a lost cause. That it was not is largely due to the efforts of Edith Moorhouse, her legendary tact, and her indefatigable work. She missed only two weeks throughout the hard winter of 1947 when the weather, which brought most of the county to a halt, made travel in her old car impossible. Once when her car ran out of petrol a mile from a school, she walked, minute books under her arm, through a blinding snowstorm and turned up looking like a snowman to the consternation and astonished delight of the teachers. With the first break in the temperature, she was off again, meeting her teachers around the 'tortoise' coke stoves of their schoolrooms and talking to them during their lunch hours, the only time when teachers could be free to discuss their problems.

She began her task by organizing group meetings, to try to break down the physical isolation of these village schools. At first she simply brought two or three neighbouring head teachers together, a remarkable experience for them in itself. Then she attracted them to seminars, to poetry readings, to talks, exhibitions and discussions. On her part, there was always the sympathetic ear, the kindness of a person who knew the problems of teaching under difficult conditions. 'Always you had to keep looking for the growth points, and never leave a teacher without feeling that something about her work was good and worth developing. The thing was to listen to them, just to listen, and try to encourage them.'

Edith Moorhouse's success in providing a link and stimulus among the schools of the county led the authority to bring in more advisory teachers, each of whom took over an area under her. This was the regional organization which Robin Tanner found waiting for him when in 1956 he came from Bristol to begin work in Oxfordshire as H.M. Inspector. It was a fortuitous but remarkable coming together of talents – the department headed by A. R. Chorlton, the field work of Edith Moorhouse and her colleagues, the recent infusion of young head teachers and the inspiration of Robin Tanner. 'The ground was prepared', as he himself acknowledged, and he moved in to build

116

upon the foundations. But his impact was far from immediate. In any case, he was absorbed in a new project.

The Ministry of Education, whose *Handbook of Suggestions for the Consideration of Teachers and Others Concerned in the Work of Public Elementary Schools* had been published as long ago as 1937, was busy producing a new primer for the primary schools created by the 1944 Act. It asked Robin Tanner to write the section on Art and Craft as well as that on Handwriting. This was more than an opportunity to record the progress of thirty years of pioneering work; it was a chance to draw up a blueprint that would go out to every primary school teacher in the country, for years to come, on what ought to be done. History it might be; propaganda it certainly was.

The chapters on Art and Craft bear the full imprint of Robin Tanner's philosophy.

The education of children should surely aim at fulfilling their creative powers as both artists and craftsmen; and at the same time it should foster their growth as discerning people, able to choose and select, to discriminate between the true and the counterfeit, to reject the shoddy and false and hold fast to that which is good – in short, to form first-hand judgements, to grow in critical awareness and in the capacity to enjoy the arts and crafts of mankind.

But there was also a warning :

This is not to suggest that boys and girls are receivers of some heavenly gift that their less fortunate teachers must be careful not to sully! On the contrary, if children are to grow to the full they need to be helped specifically and consistently to use this native language that we call Art. The teacher needs to see that it is a fundamental basis for learning and maturing. Like all forms of language, its use involves effort: there must be respect for the materials employed if they are to be properly handled as instruments of ideas. Above all, children have to be helped to observe and see; and their school environment and their experience within it should together lead them to see with a growing acuteness and discernment, with finer appreciation and subtler feeling. Children cannot be expected to grow in visual awareness unless they are taught. Their nature is such that if they are merely surrounded by attractive material and then 'allowed to develop on their own' they fail to develop but rather repeat a performance *ad nauseam* and with diminishing effort and sincerity of feeling. . . .

In Oxfordshire, Robin Tanner spent the first few years establishing himself among the schools in the county, visiting them regularly and getting to know their teachers. One young headmaster, David Evans, whose school Robin Tanner helped to transform ('It looks like a public lavatory, doesn't it?' he had said when he first saw it) described the effect of his personality :

'Robin Tanner had talked to me about William Morris, who had lived nearby at Kelmscott. I knew hardly anything about this. "Aren't you lucky," he said. "You can take your boys and girls to Kelmscott Manor and enjoy for yourselves Morris's block-printed hangings, the great Kelmscott Chaucer, and get the atmosphere of that strangely evocative house."

'But I put off going there; and then, one day, I did take the children. I shall never forget it. We set to work at once, learning about what Morris stood for, cutting and printing blocks, making books, drawing native plants like the snakeshead fritillary, and assembling a display of craftsmanship, lent by Robin Tanner and his colleagues about the work of William Morris. We just never looked back after that. We were away.

'Slowly we changed the entire appearance of our three classrooms. More than that, we changed our conception of educating children. There was not a single child who could not win some mastery over one craft or another. It was as though something of that sense of standard and of quality at the heart of Morris's way of life had communicated itself to those children. Even the infants created patterns on cloth by the age-old process of tie-dyeing, starch-resist and discharge. The younger juniors gathered wool from fences and hedges, which they carded and spun – making their own spindles, and also using an old spinning wheel. They dyed their yarns with native dye-plants which they collected, and they started to weave on looms they made themselves. The older juniors not only printed wallpapers and textiles with their own blocks, but engraved patterns on boxwood, using the tools of the adult engraver, and with these they printed cover papers for the books they made.

'What I find surprising is that each succeeding generation of children builds on and adds to this tradition that started in the late Fifties. We even have an indigo vat at school now!'

It was with young teachers like David Evans, George Baines at Brize Norton and now at Eynsham, Tom John at Tower Hill and some young women teachers that, from 1956 to 1964, Robin Tanner worked and shared his message. The message was simply that education should be designed around the child, for him, according to his nature and his needs. 'It can't be an easy path, you know,' he used to tell them. And he meant it, for what he wanted from them was a sharper awareness of the world around them, of their attitudes to young children and of their own sensibilities. Apart from encouraging ruthless honesty ('If you're really honest, you're unassailable,' he would tell his teachers), Robin Tanner achieved a great deal by bringing groups of them together, socially and unofficially. There were dinners and long talks at the Lamb Inn at Burford, where he always stayed. Or a meeting at David Evans' home at Sherborne in the Windrush valley, or a day with his family at his own home at Kington Langley, where the talk might range from ways of propagating plants, or how to make a syllabub, to a current volume of poetry, choosing a carpet, the political situation or planning a French holiday. By breaking down the insularity common to many village schools (and not only village schools!) he was, consciously or not, creating an elite among the teaching profession. For the first time, for most of these teachers, they felt part of a special vocation. 'He gave me a new dignity,' said Tom John, 'and that meant that I, in turn, gave a new dignity to the children I taught. We felt terribly important people. After all, here was one of H.M. Inspectors taking us out for poetry readings and dinners, and driving us into the country to see old churches and carvings, and sharing his own collections of art treasures with us. I wasn't being taught, exactly; I was being educated.'

A great deal of this work was done in Robin Tanner's private time, in the evenings or the week-ends. For him, there was no division of time, no 'work periods' and 'rest'. He often quoted Lawrence Binyon's line 'Nothing is enough' to prod and cajole further efforts from his team. He himself spent endless hours on his correspondence, on discovering new works of art and craft for the many displays and exhibitions that he organized in schools and colleges, and in the preparation of the many courses that he gave for educationists both in the county and at national level. In 1960, for example, he ran meetings on handwriting at Watlington, Leafield, Chadlington, Kingham, Ascot-under-Wychwood, Witney, Charlbury and Long Hanborough, and ran a course on the study of nature at Cowley Manor in Gloucestershire. The following year there was another conference on school gardens, and one on the exploration of the natural environment at Charney Manor in Berkshire. In 1962 there was one of his famous Dartington courses on 'Movement with Art and Poetry', an Oxfordshire discussion on 'Living in a New School', more poetry readings and a special celebration of William Morris.

At these conferences, the highlights were the exhibitions created, sometimes by Robin Tanner himself, and at other times with Christine Smale, one of his close colleagues. During his holidays on the Continent, he and his wife, Heather, created their private collections of baskets – their garage, where they hang from the rafters, looks like some displaced African market place – of woven and printed materials, of pots of all kinds, a vast collection of calligraphy, of books and prints, of jelly moulds, straw hats and even of corn dollies, made by countrymen from straw at harvest festivals. Christine Smale was also an avid art collector, particularly of costumes and nineteenth-century domestic craftsmanship. Together, they would start preparations for one of their exhibitions a day or so before any major course began, completely transforming the building in which it took place.

From the voluminous boot of her car, Christine Smale would produce bonnets and crinolines, early dresses of frail sprigged muslin, Victorian knick-knacks, old photographs and letters,

120

lace, velvet, feathers and brooches. From Robin Tanner's big station waggon he would haul antique and modern chairs, pictures, printed textiles, living and dried plants, baskets, wine jars, brass rubbings, eighteenth- and nineteenth-century waistcoats, prints and carvings, together with vast rolls of white corrugated card for mounting the displays. For many hours before any conference, they would be busy, with pins and rampions, placing these objects in arrangements designed to stress certain aspects of colour, design or texture.

Every member on the course would have received, some weeks before it began, a programme of suggested undertakings from which they had to choose one to pursue at the conference. A typical case was a conference held at Dartington Hall early in 1964, 'Art and Craft – Their Place in Secondary Education'. These were a few of the themes put before the teachers :

Even in the depth of winter the gardens at Dartington never look forlorn, dull, unclothed. Explore some of the many reasons for this, making numerous drawings to demonstrate your points. . . .

In the Great Hall and also in the medieval Solar a number of old, rare, costly and beautiful things are placed. There are banners, tapestries, carvings, furniture. Make a book or folio of descriptive drawings of those you like most. . . .

Study the many stone steps and stairs about the Hall and Gardens, and also the cobble and flagstone paths, particularly those in the courtyard. The stone work of the garden walls and buildings is worth noting, too. . . .

Lichens and mosses flourish in the moist, warm South Devon climate. Stone, slate, bark, wood are all friendly hosts for different kinds. Get inside this miniature world. . . .

In the architecture of Dartington, surface texture plays a significant part. Make rubbings and annotated drawings of both old and new instances – not forgetting the church tower. . . .

From the exhibition in the Great Hall make a history of English waistcoats. . . .

Such a daunting programme – there were about thirty items

to choose from – was intended to occupy only three days of a ten-day course, but if a teacher, bewildered and not a little put off by the enormity of the tasks provided, failed to produce a reasonable piece of work, Robin Tanner was never disappointed. 'It really doesn't matter,' he would say. George Baines, on his first conference at Woolley Hall in Yorkshire, began making some faltering drawings and then threw the result into the wastepaper basket in disgust. Robin Tanner pulled the crumpled paper out again, sat down with him and began to move a pencil over the work. 'I think we can probably do something here,' he said, lifting the drawing to a new and acceptable plane. George tried again, and found, as he himself later explained, that he could draw.

'You are all artists,' is how Robin Tanner would begin one of his talks to a group of teachers. He was challenged about this once from the audience. 'Really, not an artist?' he asked. 'Does someone else buy your clothes?' No, said the teacher, he bought his own. 'Well, only an artist could have bought that suit!'

During such conferences, the teachers became aware that art and craft were not merely satisfying occupations or pursuits; that behind the obvious there lay an intricate and deep philosophy which would be pursued through readings of prose and poetry, and by endless discussions on the need for and the meaning and rightness of art. ('Why do we all respond to that perfect proportion we call the Golden Mean? Why do we prefer a portrait lighted from the left? How did the inevitable shape of a spoon evolve? And why can't we tamper with it?') Robin Tanner would quote Jacquetta Hawkes, where she asked:

Where did [the makers of these flints] discover this rightness of form, a rightness we still recognize a quarter of a million years later? Did it perhaps, and does it still, spring from memories, deep in the unconscious, of natural forms observed and participated in during the vast stretches of our pre-human evolution? Is it these memories, these inherited prejudices, that make us say: this is right – the relation between this tapering point and this curving butt are so perfectly satisfying as to possess a kind of life of their own? It may be we are moved by such an inheritance, or it may be that as creatures of this world we are swayed by the laws of its construction and existence. I do not know how we come to possess them, but I am sure these aesthetic convictions of ours, these ideas of formal rightness, are bonds between the human mind and the universe in which it is lodged. They are also bonds between ourselves and our remote forebears, having passed from brain to brain, from their time until our own, in an unbroken mental process spanning all human history.*

Robin Tanner himself, stressing always the importance of quality in everything that was done for and with children, saw this strand of human consciousness as lying closest to the surface in childhood. For this reason he complained, loudly and at length, about the spuriousness and artificiality of much that was brought into primary schools. He spat out the word 'plastics' with particular venom, and once argued that the only object that had remained true to its origins in many schools was the wastepaper basket, a simple willow construction. 'But now some schools are even embroidering raffia daisies round their basket!' he exclaimed, throwing his hands in the air at the travesty. On another occasion, he threatened to write an exposé of the 'Gift Shoppes of England', for which he had a particular horror. 'The trouble is that if it were ever printed I should be prosecuted for obscene libel.'

Quality was all-important, he felt, because young children had eyes and feelings to understand and almost identify themselves with the true nature of things, and so to abuse their direct gaze was to commit a crime. That was why, he argued, a school should be a 'good place', a 'wholesome, shipshape place of truth and beauty', and every teacher, in whose trust lay the development of childhood, should be dedicated to the fight for this ideal.

It was this concern with the true, the real, the genuine that caused Robin Tanner to seek the assistance of practising artists in his contacts with teachers. Many were his personal friends, and they came willingly to help: the potters Bernard Leach, Lucie Rie and Hans Coper, the block printers Phyllis Barron

Man on Earth (The Cresset Press, 1954), p. 9.

and Susan Bosence, the architects Mary and David Medd, the craftsman-teacher Ewart Uncles, the historian Grant Uden, and the educational pioneers Dorothy and Leonard Elmhirst. All of them came to join forces, uniquely, with fellow inspectors like Christine Smale and Geoffrey Elsmore.

At the end of these gatherings, 'I felt about three feet up in the air,' one teacher remarked years afterwards. 'I was literally a changed man. It was impossible not to be. I sat down and wrote letter after letter to Robin. What about this? What about that? Should I try such and such? Why didn't we do this or that? and every time, by return of post, in the italic handwriting which he tried to instil in all of us, back would come the replies. Probably every person on the course was writing to him, too, but he always found time to write back, to keep us going. And then, perhaps four or six months afterwards, we would have a reunion. Nothing to do with the Ministry, or with his official work, but just a private social affair, where we would talk and meet him and he would keep up with events and find out how we were doing. It was a lonely business sometimes, you see. On the course, there were perhaps thirty of you all with a common purpose, but when you left with your vision, you might be the only one in your county with any idea of what you were talking about.'

As his retirement approached, Robin Tanner more than ever looked ahead to what had still to be done. 'Education has a very long tail,' he explained. 'A very long tail!' The Department of Education gave him a touching farewell, but his real send-off took place in the hall of Tower Hill School, Witney. Educationists from all over the county came to the event, and the large school hall could hardly cope with the crush.

After the tributes, he rose himself. It was an occasion when any man might have been tempted to look back. But he refused. His subject was: 'Where do we go from here?' and he drove his colleagues on with a long list of all the work that waited to be done.

'Will it ever end?' he asked them. 'No, there is no end. And that's the joy of it.'

The Forest School : 1929–38

Much of the rottenness of modern life arises from the fact that
civilization has, from the point of view of youth, made
everything 'too damned comfortable'.
Dr Ernest Westlake, *The Future Mirrored in the Past*, 1921

A few miles east of Fordingbridge, skirting the Hampshire New
Forest, and cloaked in a mantle of soaring Scots pines, there
rise a number of curious, round prominences : mounds of earth
packed around cores of ironstone. These are the Sandy Balls, a
collective name they have carried at least since the seventeenth
century. But the mounds also have individual names, and one,
Woodling Point, bears a grave.

It is a curious grave. There is no stone. Stone would look out
of place among the pine and bracken. Instead, there is a wooden
fence, knee-high, and a neat carved board, covered with a
sloping roof and carrying a Greek inscription from Sappho's
'Ode to the Even Star'.

ΦΕΡΕΙΣ ΜΑΤΕΡΙ ΠΑΙΔΑ
Here,
on Woodling Point,
overlooking his native town,
lies the body of Ernest Westlake,
1856–1922,
founder of the Order of Woodcraft Chivalry,
its first British Chieftain
and honoured as Father of the Order.
His foresight and public spirit
preserved Sandy Balls for lovers of natural beauty
and for the training of youth
in his great inspiration,
the Forest School.

Sappho's words, 'Thou bringest the child back to its mother', are appropriate. More than forty years ago, when Westlake's body was brought to this spot, educational ideas were in ferment. The First World War had created an idealism for a new order, a revolutionary movement which, for many, was inextricably linked with a return to Nature. The cities, and the capitalistic industrial complexes that bred them, were seen not only as evil in themselves, but as distorting and stunting the development of young people. To escape, to start again, to build anew : these ambitions sparked off a score of movements, some drawing on the thinking of Emerson and Thoreau and Tolstoy, others on Marx, still others on the American Indian. If we want a symbol of that time, we need only look at Edgar Rice Burroughs' famous creation, Tarzan. The king of the jungle was first published in 1914, and popularized the philosophy that nature, with its simple power ethic, embodied a nobility that was debased by modern civilization. At Whiteway in the Cotswolds, a colony of Tolstoyans started a community by buying land, burning the title deeds and living a communist existence, in which each man gave of his talents for the common good. There was a group called the Woodcraft Folk, which sought to propagate the ideals of outdoor life. There was the greenshirted Douglas Social Credit movement, and a pacifist band called the Hargreaves Group. Above all, there were the hiking and camping movements, seeking to bring young children and people out of the city slums and into the quiet and beauty of the English countryside.

It was in that countryside, among the pines of the New Forest, in 1922, that the dramatic scenes accompanying Westlake's funeral took place. Someone who was there described it like this :

'The mortal remains of the Chieftain were placed in a coffin made of the outer slabs of fir with the bark still on, and with no furniture of any kind, the usual brass handles being replaced by leather straps. In place of the ordinary coffin plate, the name ERNEST WESTLAKE was carved on the lid of the coffin, which was conveyed to Sandy Balls in an ordinary farmer's cart with no flowers covering it, but simply the orange flag – the life-giving colour – and the bright colours of his insignia of office – the Shield and Axes of the English Order.

'At the entrance to the wood all the many mourners were sent on in front, the farmer's cart with the coffin coming last, except for the close relatives and friends who followed on foot. The procession wound its way through the wonderful scenery of the wood down to the foot of the burial mount – Woodling Point – and there the coffin was unlashed and borne by six past and present members of the Order to the top of the little hillock amid the silent reverence of the large assembly.'

The occasion was full of irony. Westlake, the man of nature, died in a motor accident, one of the early victims of the age of technology. Although hailed as the father of the Forest School, the school did not take its first pupils until six years after his own funeral. And the crowds who gathered in that beautiful wood to pay their last respects to him were honouring a man who had spent a good part of his life as a recluse. He was the only child of a Quaker sailcloth manufacturer, whose wife died when Ernest was only eighteen months old. 'As soon as I got out of the nursery, I began by making platforms in trees, like the nests of the higher anthropoids, and here, high above the earth, I spent long hours swaying in the summer breezes, "the world forgetting, by the world forgot", meditating upon I do not know what, but at any rate in perfect contentment, and disdaining the grown-ups who could find happiness on the ground. This habit of tree meditation lasted throughout adolescence in the sense that, whenever I felt bored, I would run up some tree, which from long practice I could mount as quickly as a ladder; and there, sitting high up in the leafy crown and looking over the landscape, I found peace and contentment.

'I also dug out caves in the chalk, and in the sand cliffs at Bournemouth, where I suspect everything is now altogether too proper for children to have this freedom. The fascination of a cave was even greater than that of a tree, coming later and lasting longer: indeed, all through the adolescent age I felt in a cave an irresistible attraction. To explore one was, up to the age of manhood, my nearest conception of paradise. . . . Once, as I was sliding down from one of the platforms by means of an insecurely fastened rope, it came untied and I fell many feet on my nose, reducing it from a fair Roman feature to a merely Socratic one. I was carried home insensible upon a hurdle, and then my father expressed doubts about tree habitations – even though I explained that the tree was in no way at fault, but the rope which my dawning civilized proclivities had introduced.'

The young Ernest Westlake grew up in an age of immense scientific debate. Darwin's *Origin of Species* had been published when he was a baby, and the young man revelled in the 'controversy that raged about its author's head. Quiet, shy and introspective, he read widely in the scientific literature, without coming to any decision about his own future. Suddenly, in 1891, he married and had two children, but this new life as a family man was shattered when, nine years later, his wife died. It was in 1904 that Westlake decided to take his elder child, a girl, and her governess on a cycling tour of France. It was a typically unconventional idea which he thought would improve her education, but it got no further than Aurillac in the Cantal, where Westlake found a large site of eolithic stone implements. Enthusiastic about his find, he immediately settled down to work the site, and what had started as a cycling holiday became a two-year stay in France, at the end of which he had a collection of stones so large that the French Government stepped in to prevent him moving them all to England and, as officials put it, 'removing the soil of France'.

But Westlake was not to be put off so easily. He had now found his subject: palaeontology. Having briefly returned to England, he set off once more, this time for Tasmania, to make yet another collection of extinct aboriginal implements to be shipped back to England. Two years later, he was digging in the river gravel of the Hampshire Avon, as it flows around the feet of the hills that form Sandy Balls. With his collection from France, Tasmania and the Avon, he now settled down to the life of an amateur scientist, sorting and classifying, measuring and cataloguing. At fifty-eight, it looked as if he had found his life's work.

And then, in 1914, war broke out. Suddenly the solitary field scientist, absorbed in his rocks and flints, was confronted with a global challenge to the whole nineteenth-century world in which he had grown up and which he had largely accepted as representing the permanence of all things. From his studies of early man – the aborigines and the early eolithic man in France – he found himself diverted by the presence of modern man, armed with machines and guns and paper treaties, tearing himself to pieces in the mud of Flanders. What had caused this disaster? Where should one look for an explanation?

Westlake turned to the subject he knew, and thought that he saw, in primitive life's concern with the earth, with nature, with elemental forces, certain virtues that had been abandoned by the twentieth century. Man, he considered, had moved too fast and too far away from the roots that fostered him. He no longer understood his role, and in this confused state had become diseased and turned upon himself. What men should do was to return, in a sense, to the primitive, to re-educate himself into his basic humanity. Had not Darwin shown how man had emerged, as a child of nature, from the woods and the lakes? Had he not demonstrated how through natural selection, through a dynamic dialogue between nature and man, humans had refined their unique qualities and gradually won their distinctiveness? The tragedy was that this new creature had become alienated from its origins. Each succeeding generation, Westlake felt, driven onwards by ever more powerful tools, became further removed from the original concept of being, until an imbalance occurred in which man lost himself, adrift in a sea of technology.

Westlake was to live only another eight years, but during that time he transformed himself from a scientific recluse into an educationist, publisher and propagandist, heading a movement whose followers could be counted in thousands, many of them to come to Sandy Balls on that day of his funeral, to mourn someone they recognized as their leader.

He seized upon the biological theory of 'recapitulation' as expounded by the influential American psychologist Stanley Hall, in his book *Adolescence*. This claimed, among other things, that 'before birth, development is expressed in abridged series of the main ancestral forms; and though after birth this is less obvious, the recapitulation of the racial growth and experience holds true. In its growth to maturity the child recapitulates the great stages of social development in the history of the race. One after another the instinctive demands which belong to these past stages of human development arise in succession in the growing child. From this arises an important educational principle, i.e. that the child must be provided with the means to satisfy these primitive instinctive demands as they arise.'

Hall's theories do not bear much examination, but they had about them an attractive, superficial logic. Westlake recalled his own youth, climbing trees, digging caves, searching for flints, carving with stone and wood, and yes, there he saw exactly what Hall was talking about, and as he had seen it in his own intense studies of primitive man – the call of the wild, and the gradual emergence of the human spirit from its arboreal climbings to the study of Euclid and Socrates. And if this were true, if within the adolescent body of every youngster there were these yearnings to return to the origins of existence, what was to happen to them, locked away in their dingy holes in the slums of Manchester or London, oppressed by factory taskmasters and breathing the fumes of the Industrial Revolution? Westlake remembered that Darwin had commented on the iguanas of the Galapagos, fierce-looking in their natural armour, who performed ritualistic patterns of threat and counter-threat, but seldom came to physical violence. Man, on the other hand, was slaughtering himself by the millions in an apparently insane battle. The lesson was clear.

Westlake's own growing convictions were strengthened by the writings of the sociologist Professor Patrick Geddes. Geddes was disturbed by the practice – at a time of growing universality in education – of watering down the classical and academic tuition provided for a minority to the mass of children in the elementary and secondary schools. He saw these children, the sons and daughters of tradesmen, craftsmen and factory workers, losing touch with the crafts of the land and being forced to bend the knee to the academic conventions and book learning of the few. The three Rs, which before had been the creed of a small elite destined for scholarship and a life of aesthetic ease, was being offered to the masses, in which the learning of useless knowledge was superseding the natural acquisition of skills and wisdom.

The argument that Geddes used against this trend can be found today in the pages of the Newsom Committee report, and the spirit of Geddes, to make learning more relevant to the needs of the community, and of the children, has inspired every modern innovation in teaching. To redress the balance, he called for an educational programme based on the three Hs – Heart, Hand and Head. Westlake seized upon this call as a way of turning his own ideas into an all-embracing educational philosophy, in which the concept of 'recapitulation' could underpin a new approach to teaching.

'If we now ask of what that recapitulation should consist, we see that it is obviously that of the seven primitive and basic occupations. Lack of this recapitulation gives the clue to what is amiss with modern life. This recapitulatory first-hand contact with nature; this simple open-air life; the life of the wilderness, the forest, the hills and the sea, which together with his social life was the chief factor in the formation of early man, is what we know as Woodcraft.'

To bring these ideas into activity, a third element was required, and here Westlake's son, Aubrey, provided the initiative. While at Cambridge, he had taken up the new Scouting movement inspired by Baden-Powell after his experiences in the Boer War. But the idea of Scouting originally sprang from America, where Ernest Thompson Seton sought to revive the skills of the American Indian tribes by gathering young people into groups called Woodcraft Indians, and later the Woodcraft League of America. Westlake contacted Seton, studied the ideas of his movement, saw that it held all the elements associated with his own theories, and only needed adapting to British conditions to make it a fit medium for this particular crusade. Seton agreed, and the Order of Woodcraft Chivalry, with Seton as its first Grand Chieftain, was born.

Driven on by the zest of the elderly Westlake's feverish activity, this movement now emerged as a popular but rather bizarre creation. It took aboard a whole shipful of mock ritual and synthetic folklore. It had its own emblem (the red cross of St George, and two crossed axes on a white shield), its own legend ('Thou bringest the child back to its mother') and its own watchword ('Blue Sky' – taken from the American Woodcraft League). Its members were divided into troops of elves (from four to eight years old), packs of woodlings (eight to twelve), tribes of trackers (twelve to fifteen), companies of pathfinders (fifteen to eighteen) and fellowships of wayfarers (adults), grouped into Lodges and presided over by a Chief, a gleeman, a herald, a recorder, a Keeper of the Fire, a Keeper of the Honours Tally and a Keeper of the Purse. It had its own salute – 'The extended right arm is raised slowly from its normal position at the side to a position slightly inclined from the perpendicular, the palm being to the front when in that position '– and its own affirmative oath – 'To respond to the call of the world of Nature, seeking from it simplicity, good sense and fortitude. To pursue bravely and gaily the adventure of life, cherishing whatever it holds of beauty, wonder and romance; and endeavouring to carry the chivalrous spirit into daily life.'

Each group had its own uniforms, its own colour, its own set of badges. A whole language was woven around the special colour, size and complexity of shoulder knots worn on special occasions, and the rank of each member was carefully plotted according to the trials and grades which that member had undertaken and passed. Woodlings had trials of lissomness ('some suitable dance, or a bout of wrestling'), nimbleness and cleanliness. Pathfinders were faced with the Trial of Fitness, the Trial of the Thinking Hand ('Find some wild flower, make a sketch, picture or model, and from this evolve a symbolic or natural design. Then make some article on which the design can be carved, worked or painted'), the Trial of the Adventurous Rover and the Trial of the Homeland Guide. But, as in the Scouting movement to which it played rival, there were also proficiency degrees, in cooking, craftsmanship, travelling, stargazing, boating, fishing, pet-keeping, forestry, pottery and every other conceivable activity. Westlake's enthusiasm for ritual was limitless. In a series of publications which nearly all bore his unmistakable stamp, a torrent of explanatory texts, diagrams and instructions poured out to the members of the Order of Woodcraft Chivalry. There were drawings, including instructions for making the uniforms and ceremonial dress, with approximate measurements. There were laws and instructions on how to run common councils, how to administer finances, how to deal with records, how to cope with a troop of young elves. There were even detailed suggestions on the kind of ceremonial language that should be used when a new initiate was introduced to the Pack.

Pack Leader : 'Are all assembled here?'
Keeper of the Log : 'O Leader, I will take the roll.'
Pack Leader : 'Now is the time to decide who shall be of our Pack. —— there is, who would run with us. Would ye see him?'
Pack : 'Let him be shown.'

Behind all this childish but innocent nonsense, the Order was fulfilling a serious function. At the Order's Folkmoots, the Annual General Assemblies, in January 1920 and 1921, held at Shearns Restaurant, Tottenham Court Road, London (now demolished), it became obvious that a further step ahead was required. For Westlake, in his series of publications, had by now clarified the real issues. 'At a time when the voices of the prophets of the open-air life are loud in its praise as the one thing needful to combat the vices of civilization, it may seem ill-timed to insist on the fact that civilization has also its virtues. If we do so, it is not from any lack of sympathy with or underrating of savage virtue, but because we think that to point out the normal ideal of education and of life is more important than to take part in a reaction. In so far as civilization is merely something comfortable, we are very willing to throw it aside, but in so far as it has created greatness and grace in the arts and learning in the sciences, in so far as the crafts have liberated the higher energies of man, in so far as a more complex society has procured a higher morality – then to that extent we conceive the craft revolution begun in the neolithic age to have been sound, and that the clock can never be put back,' he wrote.

'We believe that the child who has been rooted and grounded in Woodcraft will be able to use the higher crafts without injury, and books without pedantry. In this way traditional learning and social culture will have full opportunity to complete the wisdom and refinement necessary to his highest functioning.'

Here one sees how Westlake conceived the Order of Woodcraft Chivalry as a particular amalgam of religion, ritual, tradition, discipline and mystical expression, all coming together in a radical movement opposed to the given social structure. This is how his son, Aubrey, interpreted it :

'The word "Order" was no accident; it was deliberately chosen to signify an organization with a very definite religious outlook, indeed Christian outlook. The Order was for him a religious movement in a profound sense. Similarly, the double title "Woodcraft Chivalry" was again no accident; while not ideal, it was the nearest he could get to expressing the essential elements in the educational programme and also the sense of balance or polarity, and indeed of wholeness, which runs through the whole of the practical expression of the Order. For example, the Order was for him not simply a children's movement, it had a place and a message for adults; it required and embraced the vigour and enthusiasm of youth, as well as the wisdom and experience of age. It was all-embracing in its age range. It included both boys and girls, men and women; both sexes being essential for balanced social and communal expression. It laid as much stress on the importance of the individual as of the group, in that they are the complementary necessity of the other. For Ernest Westlake it was the realization and enrichment of full and unique individuality which constituted the essential aristocratic counterpart of the democracy of the group, and that aristocratic reality must, he felt, have as full expression as the democratic.'

But although the theory was now complete, the reality was still far away. Westlake saw clearly that if his ideas were going to have a genuine impact, he must translate them into practice. That meant an arena, ultimately a school. But where? He combed England for a suitable site. It was just as he was despairing of finding such a place that he learnt that the family which owned some forty acres at Sandy Balls were selling the land. Westlake pounced. He had virtually no money, but to those who asked how he could possibly consider such a purchase he merely waved a scornful hand. But Westlake found himself against a powerful opponent, a local builder, who saw in the pine-covered forest a rich source of timber. The merchant offered a sum which Westlake could not contemplate, and apparently bought the property. Westlake refused to accept defeat. He drove over to the home of the builder, and by a process of charm, persuasion, and pleadings talked him into releasing his bid. The man was later to complain to Aubrey Westlake that he had no idea how he could have agreed to what he did : he was utterly unable to remember what it was that persuaded him to give up a profitable transaction of this kind. But that is what he did, and Westlake was the owner of Sandy Balls and a huge debt, something that did not deter him in the least.

And then, with this triumph behind him, with the theory of Woodcraft Chivalry laid, with four volumes of the Woodcraft Way series of books published, he returned one night from a Folkmoot, crashed, and was killed.

But the Order of Woodcraft Chivalry was by now well established, and able to survive his loss. In his death, in fact, he had given the movement its first father figure. Now it needed another, and up from its ranks it found just the man.

Cuthbert Rutter was a teacher, a man who had learnt about children in the harshest of worlds – Borstal and the London East End. He began his professional career in one of the earliest

'Borstals' near Rochester where, for about two and a half years, he was an assistant house master – one of the first of a new breed of men brought into the prison service to educate rather than to punish. With these young offenders, Rutter tried his first innovations in teaching techniques, and with a mixture of instinctive sympathy, aversion to force, and a natural talent for simplifying and dramatizing essentials he introduced them to Shakespeare and writing, to books and music and debate. After three years, Rutter was considered for a permanent and therefore pensionable position in the Borstal service, only to find his application turned down because of a weak heart.

To make his own way in his chosen profession, he left and did three weeks' trial teaching in the London East End with the object of being accepted for full training at the London Day Training College run by Professor Percy Nunn. His school was Teesdale Street Senior Boys' School in Bethnal Green. 'It seemed to me that, above all things, these boys needed action and adventure. No doubt they had not starved utterly. There are good families in Bethnal Green. Some of them are even said to possess the remarkable hereditary power of manufacturing antique furniture in their back kitchens. In Bethnal Green the rain falls, the sun shines, and the sun sets. A boy can drop his isolation; he can lose himself; he can be his gang. ... I thought that these boys should be camping, possibly hunting for some of their food, working to make their shelter, enjoying wild games of warfare in the woods. What could we do in the school room?'

Here, in the streets of Bethnal Green, was a teacher seeing and thinking about the very people who to Ernest Westlake, digging in the soils of France and Tasmania and the Avon in Hampshire, had been at the other end of theory. Rutter was little interested in 'recapitulation'. What he saw were ragged children, bullied into learning. He did not stay long. He was accepted by the college for full-time training and for the rest of his time taught some days each week at a central school for boys and girls. 'I cannot think of this school without thinking of cotton wool – not white, but grey.' On top of this already heavy workload, Rutter also took evening classes at Toynbee Hall. 'I thought at the time that as long as I could, by any means, keep awake, I could also be sufficiently alive.' At the end of his year of training, he became sub-warden at Toynbee Hall, a move which was to shape his future life. Rutter himself described what happened:

'Members of the Order of Woodcraft Chivalry made full use of the hall for meetings, dances and "wassail". The organization with this high-sounding title talked and talked and talked about starting Forest Schools. Some of us made a committee, bought an army hut and sat down solemnly in London to "have a school" in Hampshire. It didn't seem to go very well. In a residents' meeting I told of my own ideas of Forest School. Somebody remarked: "It's dreams you're dreaming – and they don't come true."

'"Very often dreams evaporate," I said, "but if we never dream anything, then nothing would happen or come true." I told the rest of the committee that I would, if they wished, give up my other ambitions and be the first headmaster of the first Forest School. The others thought that that might be the best possible way of cutting out some of the talk and getting something started. The Warden, Council and residents of Toynbee said very kind things, but I didn't feel the regret which I had felt in leaving Borstal. I had been in residence for two and a half years when, in the spring of 1930, I took up life in the army hut. We had three pupils, aged six, nine and eleven. Our chief educational facilities were access to a wood and a river.'

Just before the school began, Aubrey Westlake, Cuthbert Rutter, Norman Glaister, a friend of Westlake's, and a schoolmaster, Maurice Littleboy, launched the company which was to own the school. Its deeds were filed on 25 September 1928, with the four men as joint shareholders in the venture. Almost immediately afterwards, they produced the first prospectus:

The Forest School is inspired by the educational ideals of the late Ernest Westlake and is situated on the Sandy Balls estate in pine and beech woods on the western edge of the New Forest, overlooking the Avon valley.

The school seeks to prepare the minds and bodies of its children – girls and boys – so that they may be equipped for contact with every phase of experience of modern life.

At the Forest School the child is brought into touch with realities and is helped by a practical pursuit of the primitive arts to realize that he can learn by doing. The teaching of subjects required for examinations is not neglected, but is made subsidiary to the development of a healthy grasp of real life.

There were to be no formal classes, no standard discipline. Life in the early army hut was crude and harsh. Latrines had to be emptied by hand, a job that Rutter insisted upon doing himself. The children could attend classes if they wished, but if they were not interested in the subject, or in any school work on a particular day, there was plenty of farm work to be done on the estate, and no pressure was put on them to attend lessons. The school staff, who were labourers as much as teachers, were looked upon as group leaders, encouraging adventures and activities rather than presenting prescribed courses of study. The children had their own council, and formulated many of the rules of the community. There were no prizes for schoolwork, but 'deeds', 'honours' and 'adventures', on the Woodcraft Way principle for work well done, be it in school or on the land. The emphasis was as much on the crafts and on manual work as on the mental disciplines. A child doing music would be expected to make his own instrument. A report on one child by Rutter said of his music studies: 'Took part in percussion band and made a pipe on which he is trying to learn a tune.'

It was, in many ways, an idyllic life. The discipline could all be summarized under the headings of the three Rs: pupils must not, without permission, go on the road, the roof or the river. Apart from that, about the only point on which the school was insistent was that the children should get plenty of sleep.

It was an outdoor life, inspired by the beauty and changing seasons of the New Forest. In the autumn they saw the scarlet berries of spindlewood and butcher's broom sparkling in the

138

soft sunlight. There were puffballs to jump on, twigs to crack and gather up, pillows of dying leaves to roll in, and mushrooms to pick. In winter, they were surrounded by the stark outlines of trees bent by strong winds, with the fresh green of the hedge parsley pushing itself through the roadside banks. But it was in spring that the world really came alight. After the carpets of snowdrops and aconites, there were the wild geraniums, ground ivy and toadflax, and with them a cascade of colour from cuckoo flowers, fumitory, wood avens and water avens, betony, pale blue scabious, agrimony, valerian, lady's mantle, soapwort, vetches, angelica, hawksweed and hawkbit, goatsbeard and colts-foot. Each one of these provided a botany lesson; together they created a classroom unparalleled in its riches. Roman pottery could be dug up near the schoolhouse. Adders could be found in the woods. There were anthills in the pinewoods into which the body of a small bird or animal could be stuffed, to be picked clean and ready for skeletal observation the following day. Local farmers and villagers provided the research material for study. One market gardener revealed that the reason for the success of his prizewinning tomatoes lay in his feeding them with buckets of blood from the nearby slaughterhouse.

With such an environment, the school was able to combine the beliefs and many of the practices of the Order of Wood-craft Chivalry with the ideas of the New Education which were also inspiring other ventures like Bedales, Dartington, and Bertrand Russell's Beacon Hill School near Petersfield. The children were divided in the Order's groupings of Elves, Wood-lings, Trackers and Pathfinders. The tests which Westlake had devised, or taken from Thompson Seton were retained and used, but they were also adapted to the special needs of the school. So, for example, they might include doing sums by long divi-sion, or writing an essay on one of the Arthur Ransome books (not surprisingly, the Order's favourite author), or swimming the Avon fully clothed and righting an upturned canoe. To get into the Tracker groups, a boy had to climb an especially difficult tree in the forest called the Tracker Tree. To enter an older group a pupil had to spend a night alone in the woods, beside a fire, and write an essay describing the experience and his thoughts during the lone vigil. One boy, at the end of this particular test, reported that ants began their day at 2 a.m.

It was, as somebody once remarked, a mixture of Red Indians and Freud. The children were not always impressed by the tribal dress, the solemn oath-taking, the slightly ludicrous ritual of the Order. One little girl, writing an essay about the ceremony of Lighting the Fire, put it this way :

'Then Mary said, "Behold the fire. It leaps, it glows, it burns." What the heck would you expect, with a gallon of paraffin thrown over it!'

The staff of Forest School were poor; they were paid only £30 a year and their keep. For this they were expected not merely to teach, to encourage their young charges to dance, sing, camp out, make music and paint, but to clean the wooden school-rooms and living quarters, help with the farm work, do washing and sewing and virtually any job that needed to be done. Yet they subscribed to Rutter's view that 'to education we ought to bring the freshness of the morning. A teacher is one who enjoys a good thing and wants to share in it. A pupil is one who has an appetite and wants to satisfy it. But by the time we have organized schools, we are fortunate if such simplicities have not evaded us.'

Sometimes the school, in its zeal for reform, was led into absurdities. Following the methods designed for the Order of Woodcraft Chivalry, some of the teachers re-baptized themselves with Red Indian names like Great Bear, Rising Sun, Laughing Water, Otter and Golden Eagle. The bank manager in the neighbouring village of Fordingbridge, asked to meet payment on cheques signed 'Great Bear' and 'Otter', sighed : 'What have you got up there? A menagerie!'

But the school itself was a serious attempt at educational reform. It was partly inspired by the points raised by Professor Findlay in a book called *The Children of England*. In this he emphasized that schooling, which had previously been given to embryo priests and professional men, had only been extended to the mass of children as a means of escape from work. Having accepted that factories were no place for children, they had been put into school instead, without any thought being given to what school was supposed to do for them, or they at school. Forced to define their terms, authorities had assumed that schooling meant the acquisition of knowledge, just as had always been the case, and that for those who now found themselves 'being educated' hard work and fact-learning was imperative.

'And so we come to the revolt of the modern educationists against the appalling waste of physical and mental energy amongst children compelled to spend their time upon occupations in which they have no interest. It is again to rescue them from work, this time the work of the schools instead of the factory, that the zeal of the reformer is kindled,' wrote one Forest School enthusiast.

Inspired by a kind of missionary fervour, the Forest School staff tried to provide for their charges an environment that was a kind of amalgam between a camp, a school and a Scout jamboree. It is fair to say that the mixture never truly set. In some way, ambitions overran resources. In another sense, one might ask how much the enterprise was for the benefit of the children, and how much of it was of therapeutic value to the staff. Probably it was intended to be both. But in the character of Cuthbert Rutter, these contradictions were clearly apparent. Privately, he was a very introspective man. All his life he kept small black diaries in which he analysed his own feelings, and came back, again and again, to significant episodes in his own childhood that caused him distress or doubt. His insistence upon doing the most menial and unpleasant chores himself – like the latrine duties – was partly inspired by a selfless devotion to his responsibilities. But they were also more than that, a sort of spiritual purging not unlike that which T. E. Lawrence inflicted upon himself after Deraa.

One mother of two children who went to the school described her own impressions with great clarity and honesty. She was hardly an unbiased witness, for she was the wife of Aubrey Westlake, the school's chairman. 'One of its main disadvantages as far as my two children were concerned was its size. A handful of boarders of all ages, all individualists, and some of them problem children, cared for by too small a staff, who had to be jacks of all trades, although I do not mean to imply that they were master of none. The change from large classes of the same age group to almost individual age grouping was keenly felt. The woods, and the more adventurous and hardy outlook on life, partly compensated for this loss, but I know my daughter was lonely and eventually we took her away because of this. But not before it was evident that the Forest School, with its insistence on learning by doing, its encouragement of initiative, hardihood and self-reliance, had a very real and constructive lesson to teach sincere and forward-thinking educationists.

'For one whole summer term I was at the school as house-mother, doing the cooking, washing and looking after the younger children, so I had first-hand experience of the life. Its keynote was simplicity and a deep belief in the importance of learning by doing. There was very little equipment, so the fullest possible use was made of the natural resources of the place. The children climbed trees, made houses in them, using bracken and boughs. They played in a large, natural sandpit at the back of the house, and dug clay from a seam in the back, from which they made elementary pots and persuaded me to bake them in the oven. They never tired of the streams and the river or of exploring the wood and the edge of the New Forest. Lessons and meals were out of doors whenever possible.'

This mixture of the open-air life, at once school and camp, played tricks on memory. One former pupil, writing in the Forest School Camps magazine, admitted as much : 'I find it difficult now to separate school from the camp, and the memories of one from memories of the other. Some are easy, of course. The midnight battle between two bands creeping through the bracken of the New Forest, that belongs to the camp. Latin taught by Leslie England in a bathroom because it was the most peaceful place in the school (I learnt it reluctantly and alone, but necessarily for Common Entrance), that belongs to the school. But did we ride New Forest ponies through the woods at night at camp as well as at school? If not, who looked after them?

'It is the kindliness and the laughter and the tolerance that principally remain in the memory. Somewhere along the line one learnt to read a map and pitch a tent and cook on a wood fire in the rain. These skills could have been learnt elsewhere, I suppose, but what Forest School had to offer was in those days unique.'

Mrs Westlake's own conclusion was similar. 'Life today is becoming increasingly uncertain and insecure and particularly difficult for the young. Victorian education – to which we still largely adhere – was education for a stable future. What is urgently needed now is education for an uncertain, unstable, sometimes almost hypothetical future, and this cannot be acquired or superimposed in a day. The aim of educationists should be to fit children for anything they may have to meet, not coerce them into a stereotyped pattern.'

Sadly enough, the school which set out to provide this kind of training was itself not destined to survive change. It became increasingly obvious that, as the danger of war came nearer, the site of the school would have to be changed. By 1938, the New Forest site had been given up in favour of an apparently better school building at Whitwell, near Reepham in Norfolk, some twelve miles from Norwich. Cuthbert Rutter was still the headmaster, and his wife, Helen, remained the house mother, but a number of other staff failed to make the transition from Hampshire to Norfolk, and it was obvious to everyone that the coming war would soon end the Woodcraft experiment. By 1940 the school was closed, and its buildings taken over for the war effort.

Rutter, although he was by this time a weak, sick man, continued to teach, first at the Nottingham High School, and then in Kent at a senior elementary school. 'I helped my boys to feel that life in the classroom was really life and that it was theirs. "Good Heavens!" you may think, "if you can't do such a simple thing you can't begin to teach." Quite true. But you would cry if you knew how often this elementary thing is not achieved. For sometimes it is hardly attempted. Not infrequently it is despised.'

In a letter to a friend in 1945, he described his war effort 'in three short paragraphs'. It is a remarkable document for its brevity in no way dims the essential driving force that had founded Forest School. Characteristically, he undervalued himself. 'I had far too little understanding of the special problems and war-time lives of my pupils,' he wrote. 'Nevertheless I did help them quite a lot to live and grow. I was richly blessed. Also I was worn out. I easily get worn out.'

Then he added a postscript, in which his enthusiasm for the original project swept back again. 'And yet I know that I have something to contribute and I hope that my little strength will thus be best used. Forest School has been evacuated by the army. When it re-opens I hope to help on committee and in work behind the scenes.'

But soon after, Rutter was dead. When the doctors operated on him, they found that his weak heart was almost twice the size of a normal one. To his friends, it seemed, somehow, a biological verification of the man.

Henry Morris: 1889–1961

... The town and countryside must be planned so that they will provide a way of life (the new democratic way of life). The alternative is more barbarism and militarism. I think that we might lead the world here. The reactionaries say that democracy cannot evolve a culture and will not know how to use the artists. We have to disprove this.

Henry Morris, 1945

In the early 1940s, some of the more optimistic intellectuals and administrators were already plotting a peace-time offensive on an education system that had failed to live up to the ideals of a democratic society. One of them was Henry Morris, Chief Education Officer of Cambridgeshire, who was invited in September 1942 to explain his ideas on the B.B.C. North American Service. He was introduced as 'one of the present-day revolutionaries in British education' and in the space of about ten minutes he provided the best available account of his philosophy and ambitions:

'For twenty years,' he said, 'I have been working at my job as an educationist fired by the belief that the school in England, indeed in every country in the world, has to be remade; and I know that millions of ordinary men and women in all countries, looking back on their childhood, think the same. What has been wrong and what is still largely wrong? First of all the object of the school everywhere has been dominated by the exceptional needs of the "brainy" boy or girl who is good at books and comes out well in written examinations and who wins the prizes at the universities. Now these boys and girls are a minority in every country, though a precious minority – in England they are between five and ten per cent of all boys and girls in schools. Even for them this academic education is not wide enough. And for the millions of boys and girls who learn by practice and by action it is a gigantic error. Secondly, the

145

characteristic fallacy of adolescent education everywhere in the world is that teachers try to teach the boy and girl subjects and ideas which are more fitted for adult life – both in science, the arts and religion. Of course the education ought to be given in terms of the experience and instincts of adolescence. Thirdly, the main instrument of education in the School everywhere has been discourse by word of mouth and based on books. Schools have been classroom-ridden, lesson-ridden, textbook-ridden, information-ridden.

'How is all this to be corrected? The answer is slowly taking shape in many countries. . . . In England, which I know best, the Senior School is showing the way in town and country.

'What is the secret of the Senior School seen at something like its best? I cannot do better than take you to a country school a few miles from the University Town of Cambridge – the Village College of Impington, designed by the great architect Walter Gropius, now Professor of Architecture at Harvard University.

'The secret of the Senior School is activity – the major road to knowledge both for children and grown-ups. Here the dismal reign of mere chalk and talk, of the mechanical use of the textbook and the piling-up of parrot facts unrelated to the child's experience is finished. The school has become a society with a way of life. On any morning of this fateful summer you would see the boys and girls coming from ten villages on foot, on bicycle or bus, 350 of them full of zest. The morning assembly is a cheerful affair bright with music and hymns with the Bible lesson read by a pupil. Within a few minutes you would see the school becoming a hive of constructiveness. One group is in the six-acre garden with its adjacent laboratory and greenhouse. Here all kinds of vegetables and fruit are grown for experiment and demonstration. Seeds and manures are tested, pigs, poultry and bees are cared for and fed. accounts and records are carefully kept, flower gardens and lawns are beautifully tended. It is a school estate in which the simplest boy in due course can acquire for life an understanding of a fundamental scientific law that affects all living experience – the law of cause and effect.

'Come to the wood and metal workshops. Here boys, and girls too, are making real things for the house and the garden, using what has been well called the "thinking hand". Thus they satisfy a manual instinct as old as the human race. Furthermore they learn the more surely how to measure, how to add, subtract and multiply, because all these mathematical operations are given meaning and reality. Again in the rooms for cookery and housewifery and infant welfare vital needs and instincts are the medium of training. Note another point of interest. It is that history and geography start out from the history and geography of the surrounding countryside – from its industries, its agriculture, its geological formation, its rivers, its plant life, its beasts, birds, moths and butterflies. . . .

'Impington Village College is a Community Centre of the Arts where children can consume and enjoy cooperatively all the art forms which otherwise would be impossible. One of the most interesting sights is a group of boys and girls doing rhythmic dancing under the leadership of Mr Kurt Joos, whose ballet is as famous in America as it is in Europe. Another is to hear music played or sung by orchestra and choir; another to see the dramatic act done sometimes to make more vivid a great point of history, or for the delight of the spoken word and the dramatic situation.

'Let me come to a favourite theme of mine. I always feel that the midday meal can be one of the most significant incidents in the life of the Senior School. The common meal has been one of the main instruments of education in civilization east and west. The common meal is not an extra at Impington. It has a place of honour in the curriculum. The tables are charmingly set out, there is a fine sung Grace, the children sit together with their teachers, there is an interval between the courses (a great artist said "slowness is beauty"), at the end there is music or a reading. Here is a scene of happiness, gaiety and health. A boy or girl who has sat through these common meals for four or five years will have acquired sound food habits for life and a fund of good manners.

'The Senior School can thus provide for the mind and the

147

emotions, and for the play and exercise of body which youth demands. What of the spirit and religion? The Senior School at Impington tends to make even religion a thing of reality for the adolescent and that cannot be done by preaching and exhortation. The Senior School must be a society in which the growing boy and girl have hourly and daily opportunities of *practising* in a way they can understand what have been finely called the *actions* of religion, in particular cooperation, unselfishness, helpfulness, kindness, affection, trust. We fail miserably when we try to educate boys and girls under eighteen in the methods appropriate to men and women of twenty-one to thirty, and in no sphere is it truer than in religious education. . . .

'I must close with a note at once both of counsel and of prophecy. The school is not enough. Indeed a good deal, perhaps a major part of what we have done in the school, may be lost unless we do something more. We begin to enter more fully into the world of reality at the age of sixteen, and the golden time for education, especially self-education, which is the most real form of education, is between the ages of sixteen and thirty. Every country in the world needs a fully developed system of adult education. Universal adult education is, I believe, the one way available by which humanity can begin effectively to solve its problems and to make civilization a success. In England and in America it is being realized that the school should be part of a community purpose and programme, both in the country and the town. This is not an idle dream. In my own county of Cambridge all our Senior Schools are designed as part of a community centre serving a rural region. . . . Impington, for instance, is designed so that all its workshops and laboratories can be used by both adults and adolescents, but apart from these there is special accommodation set apart for adults, lecture rooms, library, billiard rooms, committee rooms, common room and canteen. You may go there any evening and, though there is a war on, you will find some hundreds of young people and parents enjoying a general programme of lectures, crafts, games, dance, cinema or simply sitting in the common room over a cup of coffee and a magazine. The Senior School here is indeed not isolated but part of a community pattern. That blueprint is, I believe, valid for the countryside everywhere. Indeed, I hold that all town and country planning ought to have as its final object the cultural and recreational life of the adult community.

'Such in brief is Impington. I said to one of the boys, "How do you like this?" "Oh, Sir," he replied, "It's fine. It's so much better than school!" '

Henry Morris is traditionally and rightly associated with the original conception of village colleges – schools that at the same time are centres for community activities – which he established in Cambridgeshire. But stated baldly and without an understanding of the personality of the man it is impossible to conceive of the impact of his ideas. He possessed two outstanding characteristics: he loved beauty – in music, art, literature and architecture; and he attracted talent like a top flight festival of culture. What other education officer could claim to have initiated a school designed by Walter Gropius and Maxwell Fry? Yet he was not a "creative artist" in any normal sense of the phrase.

There were other paradoxes in his life. He came from a moderately prosperous Lancashire family but refused to talk of his home background and made no effort to correct the fanciful stories that circulated about the money raised to send him to Oxford. It was said that a wealthy old lady had financed him through university or, alternatively, a clergyman had provided the capital. It is true that an older friend in the church, who was doubtless impressed by Morris's fond regard for clerical ritual, encouraged him – unsuccessfully – to take holy orders. In fact, his education was subsidized by his family, who received scant recognition for their sacrifice. His mother died in 1905 when he was sixteen, but his father, three brothers and four sisters survived and he succeeded in losing contact with every one of them.

He liked to pose as the natural born aristocrat. He was generous with his own money (occasionally) and other people's (frequently), inwardly disdainful of those who imagined they held some authority over him and alternately kind and demanding in his relations with the select few whom he regarded as his equals. He devoted his entire life to the purpose of raising the educational standards of the mass of the population not blessed with wealth or exceptional abilities. But he remained very much 'the Leader' – and at first assessment it is difficult to imagine how such an aloof personality managed to win fanatical loyalty from his employees in administration and in the schools.

The truth is that Henry Morris was not only a brilliant man, he was also an outrageous man. His opponents were the conservatives – prominent aldermen, civil servants, heavy-weight educationists – and he fought his battles in the grand manner with a mental agility and wit that defied retaliation. Those of his contemporaries who were on his side could not help but admire and recognize him as an outstanding ally.

His studies at Oxford were interrupted by the First World War, but during his two years at the university he developed a strong interest in education. The dominant influence on the shaping of his philosophy was his tutor, Hastings Rashdoll. In particular, Rashdoll's book *Universities of Europe in the Middle Ages* appealed to what, at this stage, was Morris's cosy sense of paternalism, and he fastened on to the concept of establishing educational institutions in rural areas that could act as guardians and dispensers of learning for the uninitiated adult population.

When the war ended he was a captain in the R.A.S.C. He had seen and experienced fighting in France and Italy. Not unnaturally the violent interlude soured his taste for the existing education system which had failed as a civilizing power. Until the end of his life the constant emphasis on the need to develop creative, artistic, scientific and moral abilities was reinforced by the terrible image of 'men hanging on the wire'!

He completed his education at King's College, Cambridge, where he read moral science for four terms and obtained a second-class degree in 1920. Haig's armies had consumed a high proportion of the young talent in the universities and when Morris decided on a career in educational administration there was a surplus of jobs open to him. He spent a year in Kent as assistant secretary to the Education Committee and then moved back to Cambridgeshire – still as an assistant. In 1922 at the age of thirty-three, he was appointed Education Secretary for the county.

It was no accident that he chose administration in preference to teaching. He was a man of ideas and he wanted the authority to implement his plans. More important, his interest in children was purely secondary to his ambitions for the development of adult education. When he argued that youngsters under the age of sixteen were unable to appreciate many of the finer things in life, he was rationalizing his capacity to understand more clearly the potential abilities of the older mind. Although he served the interests of children better than most education officers of his generation, he was awkward and shy in their company and lacked the facility to converse at their level. On one occasion, when he was escorting a party of county councillors and clerics on a tour of the junior schools, he was horrified to discover that the Bishop of Ely preferred to play games with the children than to listen to a passionate tirade on the aims of modern education. Morris summoned his car and the guests were hurried on to their next appointment.

From the very early days in Cambridge he established a reputation as the Max Beerbohm of the education world. He appeared at the office in a bright tie – usually blue, yellow or red – yellow braces and, occasionally, an eye-dazzling scarlet suit. In his flat above a book shop he was said to dine by candlelight. He surrounded himself with eighteenth-century furniture and his books – classical literature, philosophy and especially poetry.

'I am reading much,' he wrote in 1936, 'even Gibbon! – and much poetry. I often wonder why one has this undeviating passion for poetry : mainly because the visual arts were a later acquirement. I had much music before sixteen, but poetry still has the preference.'

151

Music was one of his favourite relaxations, and Mozart was his favourite composer. To establish rapport with the works of the great man was, thought Morris, a mark of intellectual distinction. Speaking of the appointment of a clerk, to a committee member who thought the successful candidate 'somewhat limited', he retorted : 'One can hardly expect a Mozartian for £300 a year!'

He never married and his friendships extended chiefly to men. In a more permissive society he might have emerged as a homosexual, but instead he talked a great deal about the sublimation of the sex impulse – by which he meant the transference of sexual vitality into intellectual channels.

He liked to have people around him, and when he rented a house called the Old Granary which overlooked the river he was able to invite groups of friends for weekend parties. It was from this home that he would set out on his famous ten-mile walks. One of his companions on these endurance excursions recalls him '... swinging wildly his ash-plant stick and carrying a battered rucksack on one shoulder, sometimes plodding through heavy rain. Accompanied or followed in twos or threes by enthralled or talkative friends, he would launch out on some favourite topic, emphasizing his words from time to time with wild swipes at imaginary *bêtes-noires*, or obstructions, or animals. I remember a disquisition on architecture and gardens which took place in a pub. As we left, a concrete statue of a gnome caught Henry's eye, and in the heat of the moment, and with a suitable oath about 'mass-produced non-art', he raised his stick and nearly severed the offending object's head. He was as astonished as the owner at this only half-intended result.'

It is impossible to guess how much he absorbed of the discussions with his widening circle of friends, many of whom were already influential in their own artistic spheres. But his ideas on educational reform were quickly germinating and by 1924 he was ready to submit his plans to the test of public and official criticism.

One of the university organizations to which Henry Morris

attached himself was the Adult Education Group. The Chairman was St John Parry, Vice-Master of Trinity College and a member of the Committee that produced the Reconstruction Report on Adult Education in 1919. Morris enthusiastically joined in the discussion on what provisions ought to be made by local authorities, and solicited views on his own scheme for the creation of village colleges.

Sometime in 1924 he spent a week at Belbury Manor in Oxfordshire, the home of Robertson Scott, who edited *The Countryman*. It was here that he drafted a pamphlet called *The Village College*. Subsequently in speeches and articles he advocated that local authorities should be required to set up '... cultural institutions that are both centres of every form of adult education and community centres with every kind of social and recreational facility'. In rural areas '... the solution will take the form of ... centres that house the senior or multi-lateral school in the day time', but in the industrial conurbations where '... further overcrowding ... is unthinkable', there was first of all a need for the Government to solve the problem of congestion by instituting a policy of decentralization and dispersal.

His critics dismissed him as a futuristic idealist and even some of his friends regarded him as a man born before his time. But, ironically, most of his thinking was rooted in the lessons of the past:

'The unity of social and spiritual life with its institutional and civic expression in architecture and organization which was characteristic of the medieval town and the parish church and manor of the countryside has gone for good and all. But the effect, in modern times, of pluralism of associations and beliefs has been one of social disintegration, less evident in the village than in the contemporary town with its ... architectural chaos. Since the breakdown of the Catholic civilization we have, so far as the social expression of values in communal living is concerned, been living on credit, consisting of the legacies of the forms of the Middle Ages and of the brief and brilliant, but morally impossible, eighteenth century.'

The cultural breakdown resulting largely from the decay of religious sanctions and aggravated by the increase of leisure was evidenced '. . . in the addiction, terrifying in its proportions, to commercialized amusements, football pools, dog-racing, watching professional sport, with all the accompanying betting, to the passive pursuit by day and night of the films and wireless, to cheap newspapers and, in recent times, to astrology. Other aspects of it are the great aimless crowds in the streets and the public houses at the weekends; the acceptance as normal by the greater part of society of the hideous squalor of our towns; and the many thousands who live in the long streets put up by the speculative builders, who seem to be known only to the rent collectors and the undertaker. Finally, there is the epic dullness and malaise of some hundreds of industrial and country towns with no corporate tradition of cultural activity and amenity.'

Like a historian of the 'Merrie England' type, Morris was inclined to ignore the serious deficiencies, both spiritual and physical, of the medieval community, and he was hard in his criticisms of the first painful strugglings of the technological society. But he clearly recognized that: '. . . we have to find a principle of integration which will allow unity of communal life and architectural expression and at the same time give free development to that pluralism of associations on which growth and freedom depend. In medieval Europe a common organization for communal living was made possible by a system of common values and beliefs. In our time that element of unity in the life of society which is essential will be attained by the organization of communities around their educational institutions. It is by some such synthesis that modern communities can again become significantly organic, that the decay of civic life and architecture can be arrested, and the planning of modern towns on lines of imaginative significance surpassing the achievement of the past, be made possible.'

Later in 1924 Morris was invited to meet Lord Eustace Percy, Parliamentary Secretary to the President of the Board of Education, and he sprang at the chance to persuade a junior minister to help and encourage the village college idea. He decided to stay with friends in London overnight, and on the morning of the appointment he was helped into what he petulantly described as his 'administrative collar', a stiff white one with wings. The interview was a failure from the moment of the first handshake. Not unnaturally, the scope of the conversation was limited by the Government's paranoiac preoccupation with the need for Exchequer economy, but Percy's opening remarks – 'Well now, what is this little bubble we must prick' – might have been phrased more tactfully. Morris was furious and indignant that 'Lord Useless Percy' had not immediately recognized and accepted his plans. This was his first experience of administrative and political obstruction. He was never fully reconciled to the rule of the game that no innovation is allowed an easy passage, but he learned to overcome his disappointments by shutting them entirely from his mind and loudly insisting to anyone who cared to listen, 'There must be no regrets for the past.'

At about this time, John Reith, the newly appointed managing director of the British Broadcasting Company, invited him to join the organization as director of education. The post was potentially influential and, for those days, highly remunerative. An initial salary offer of £1,500 was raised to £2,000, and this was at a time when Morris earned no more than £600 in his capacity as Chief Education Officer. Reith's determination that broadcasting should bring into the home '... all that is best in every department of human knowledge, endeavour and achievement' was very much in accord with Morris's philosophy and it is not altogether clear why he refused the opportunity to work with a powerful new medium. There was some discussion on the question of security of employment but this was not a factor that was likely to worry Morris and he probably used it simply as a bargaining weapon in the negotiations. More likely, Morris recognized the possibility of a clash of personalities. Both men were roughly the same age, possessed strong opinions and were inclined to autocratic methods to achieve their objects. In the Cambridgeshire of the 1920s, Morris was a big fish in a little pool. This was the life he preferred and he might reasonably have calculated that he stood a better chance of transforming the country into 'a demonstration area for rural reconstruction' than of taking the British Broadcasting Company by storm.

His first aim was to convince the Education Committee and the Council that his ideas were something more than idle theorizing. By the nature of their environment, rural councillors are instinctively conservative in their attitude to matters of social reform and in the 1920s, with the agricultural slump and the upheaval in the traditional class structure, an education officer who was intent upon introducing sweeping changes was really more than they could tolerate. During one particularly frustrating and angry exchange with his Committee, a friend suggested, not very seriously, that he might submit his resignation.

'Good God,' said Morris, 'I couldn't do that, they would accept it.'

The opponents of the village colleges relied chiefly on the argument that the scheme was impracticable financially. Provisions for adult education and recreation were not eligible for Exchequer grants and not even Henry Morris could persuade the electors to pay higher rates for the privilege of sponsoring an East Anglian renaissance. Morris overcame the problem by appealing for private donations.

It took five years for the first village college to be constructed. It was built at Sawston, where the Spicers, a prominent local family, sympathized with Morris's concept of education to the extent of offering £1,200 for the purchase of materials. The Carnegie Trust was persuaded to grant £5,500 and there were many other smaller contributions to cover everything from 'a system of aeration', electric installations and a piano to a fountain in the court. The total estimated cost was £15,300. (The final bill was over £21,000.) Without appearing mean or stubbornly retrograde, the Education Committee had no choice but to offer their support. By winning such reputable converts as the Carnegie Trust, Morris had increased his own stature. He was now the respectable revolutionary. In any case, the Council had to find little more than half the estimated expenditure and roughly fifty per cent of that was covered by Exchequer grants.

Even before the completion of Sawston, Morris was working hard to persuade the 'sometimes reluctant, sometimes hostile' County Council to approve a scheme for the establishment of village colleges throughout the county. His success with the Carnegie Trust encouraged him to aim higher with his latest money-raising campaign. His target was the Spelman Fund of New York, a research and charitable foundation which was actively involved in the improvement of public health services and particularly interested '... in securing continuity of medical supervision from birth through the whole school career and into the adult stage'. It was an ideal for which Morris had strong sympathy and, in drawing up the plans for five new village colleges, he combined expediency with a social conscience to provide the Spelman Trustees with every possible incentive to cooperate.

'We propose ... to make a special feature of the health services, of health education and health propaganda. ... We shall begin with the expectant mother and thus have a maternity centre. We shall pay special attention to the pre-school child (of whom the Chief Medical Officer of the Board of Education says that from one quarter to one third on their admission to school at the age of five are "damaged goods" needing immediate medical attention to serious constitutional impairment that could have been prevented by advice and treatment) by means of a combination ... of the functions of the day nursery, the nursery school, and the infant welfare centre. We shall make the treatment of the school child between five and fifteen more effective because the school nurses will be in constant attendance at the school clinic. We shall be able to bridge the mischievous gap in the medical supervision of adolescents between fourteen and sixteen. The schoolgirl will learn about infant welfare and domestic science before she leaves school; mothers will get to know not only how to bear and rear healthy infants, but in the domestic science centre, which will take the form of a rural worker's cottage, they will learn in day and evening classes how to keep their families healthy by proper feeding and by the hygienic care of their homes. In the gymnasium which will be contrived in the Hall and on the recreation field, physical training and games will be available for the young and the mature.'

The Spelman Fund offered £45,000 on condition that the rest of the money (about £80,000) could be raised elsewhere. For Morris it was an incredible achievement which involved months of letter-writing and discussion. But even with such a powerful backer he needed to tap additional sources of private revenue. Two anonymous donors gave £1,000 when they were persuaded that the village colleges would benefit agricultural education. A local foundation promised £850 and the Buxton Trust subscribed £200. When the contributions were totalled, and Exchequer grants, the use of sites and materials already owned by the authority and the proceeds of the sale of disused school buildings were taken into account, it was calculated that the Council would need to find the then extravagant sum of £45,000 to cover their share of the costs.

Official sanction might have been held up indefinitely had not the policy of the Board of Education moved over to the lines on which Morris was working. The pace was slower but the direction was right. C. P. Trevelyan, the Minister of Education in the Labour government of 1924, was committed to the ideal of 'secondary education for all' (the title of a party pamphlet by R. H. Tawney) and he instructed his consultative committee, headed by Sir Henry Hadow, to consider the legislative and academic framework within which the local authorities would have to work.

The Hadow Report was published in 1926 and it recommended that the school leaving age should be raised from fourteen to fifteen and that the concept of secondary education be extended beyond the type of academic course provided by grammar schools to cover 'modern secondary schools' where the instruction could be given a 'practical' bias. This meant the complete reorganization of the elementary schools – where the majority of children remained from the age of five to fourteen –

since the Report urged that there should be a 'break at eleven' when pupils would transfer from the primary to the secondary stage of education.

By 1926, the Conservatives had returned to power and the raising of the school leaving age was shelved. But the long process of reorganization was got under way and the building programme was expanded to allow for the construction of the new secondary schools. In some areas, including Cambridgeshire, there was a strong movement in favour of saving money simply by adapting existing facilities. Morris hotly opposed the compromise and emphasized time after time that the '... reorganization of elementary education – an opportunity which will not occur again – should form part of a scheme for organizing community centres affecting every side of rural welfare.'

The Board of Education was inclined to take his side and even Lord Eustace Percy, now Minister of Education, who had earlier gone out of his way to discourage Morris, visited the county and told an audience: 'I look forward to something in the nature of local colleges in rural districts grouping and focusing all the various educational and social activities together and really providing intellectual leadership and intellectual education for all the workers of the countryside.' In April 1927 the Education Committee approved a scheme for the establishment of village colleges throughout the county.

Three years later, Sawston Village College, originally sponsored in 1925 as an isolated experiment, was officially opened by the Prince of Wales. For Morris it was the greatest event in his life. Thousands of people gathered for a lavish ceremony to set the seal of establishment approval on the community centre and to pay tribute to the '... vision, energy and enthusiasm' of the chief instigator. He deserved his party.

Years later his friends clearly understood what Sawston meant to him when he unemotionally paraphrased Churchill: 'I gave my blood for Sawston,' he said. 'Not my sweat. My blood.' At about the same time (1944) a newly appointed clerk in the education office remarked, 'Mr Morris is very handsome and impressive.' 'You should have seen him in the early days,' replied one of the old guard. 'You should have seen him at the opening of Sawston Village College. He – was – *magnificent*.'

Sawston rapidly achieved the notoriety of an educational showpiece. The facilities were unrivalled and the six villages within the catchment area – which for the purpose of self-improvement were linked by a free bus service – gave the college unqualified support. Henry Morris had the problem of finding staff who understood his aims and were prepared to devote more time and energy to the job than the average teacher; but the prestige of the place attracted talent. One observer commented, 'The belittlers have never been able to employ the most devastating criticism of all – "It does not work".'

Plans were prepared for two more village colleges at Bottisham and Linton, but their construction was delayed by the slump and they were not ready for use until 1937. The interval gave Morris the chance to reconsider his attitude to school architecture and design. He recognized the need to get away from the sombre environment of the Victorian mock-Gothic institutions, but when the plans for Sawston were prepared he lacked appropriate advice and the style of the building was in the eighteenth-century symmetrical tradition. Though not externally offensive, it could hardly be described as a major breakthrough in educational architecture.

His experience in the 1930s entirely altered his approach to school design. In 1929 and again in 1932 he visited the United States and Canada, the second occasion on the proceeds from the sale of copies of the Cambridgeshire Religious Syllabus which he had compiled eight years earlier. The purpose of his journeys was to assess the developments in American rural education; but the chief benefit to Morris was the opportunity to see how contemporary architecture allowed teachers greater freedom and flexibility in the organization of their classes.

He returned to the United States in 1934, this time at the invitation of the trustees of the Spelman Fund, who wanted him as an adviser for a twenty-five-million-dollar federal scheme for the setting-up of rural community centres. Progress at home was painfully slow and in some quarters a suspicion was prevalent that Morris would prolong his stay in a country where the government was less parsimonious in its attitude to public investment. For instance, the *New Statesman* complained that:

His schemes for improving and extending [the village college project] in other zones were frustrated by the crisis, aided by the opposition of local vested interests. But where his own countrymen were hesitant a foreigner of vision has pounced, and while the educational lights of Cambridgeshire are still rubbing their eyes and wondering what to do with this strange fellow, President Roosevelt has hauled him off to America. ... I gather Mr Roosevelt thinks the job should take him three months, though I should not be surprised if he stayed there longer. I hope, at any rate, that when the prophet returns to his own country he will not continue to be without honour.

The prophet spent no longer than his allotted period in the United States and soon after he reoccupied his office in Cambridge, work began on the village colleges for Bottisham and Linton. Their design proved that Morris had finally disassociated himself from the past. At Bottisham the local residents waited and watched with some curiosity as a building laid out like a C slowly took shape. The main block contained the hall and the adult common room and lecture hall which connected with a circular library. The main hall was designed to cater adequately for morning assemblies, midday meals, plays, concerts and, in wet weather, physical training. Extending from the north-west corner of the hall was the senior school wing, planned on an arc of a circle with almost continuous ranges of windows opening southwards on to the playing fields. One critic described the architecture as 'functional' and though technically accurate the word projects a harsh image which detracts from the pale tones of the bricks and the flat outlines of the roofs that harmonized with the smooth contours of the surrounding landscape. Inside the college a variety of cheerful colour schemes enabled the students to escape from the clinical environment of grey walls and white tiling that depressed the energy of most of their contemporaries. Morris's experience in America was supplemented and reinforced by influences at home. His friend,

Jack Pritchard, a business man, engineer and economist who was instrumental in commissioning original designs for furniture and buildings, persuaded him that there was a real need for an art expression which looked to the present and the future for its inspiration. He introduced Morris to some of the best creative minds of the pre-war generation, including Henry Moore, Wells Coates and Walter Gropius, who was helped by Pritchard to leave Germany when the Nazi leaders pursued the doctrines of racial purity and intellectual degradation to their terrifying conclusion. Gropius was the founder and director of the Staatliches Bauhaus, or School of Architecture, in Dessau where artists, scientists, designers and technologists combined their talents and experimented with ideas for creating consumer products that were capable of meeting every commercial, technical and aesthetic requirement.

'... Our guiding principle,' he wrote, 'was that artistic design is neither an intellectual nor a material affair, but simply an integral part of the very stuff of life. ... Our object was ... to liberate the creative artist from his other-worldliness and re-integrate him into the workaday world of realities; and at the same time to broaden and humanize the rigid, almost exclusively material mind of the business man.'

Morris was immediately attracted to a philosophy that embraced so many of his own ideas. He was determined that Gropius should design the next village college at Impington, but the architect was thought to be wildly unorthodox and the minority who were aware of his achievements and recognized his potentialities were not represented in Cambridgeshire. The Education Committee bluntly refused to pay the fees and Morris and Jack Pritchard realized that they had either to raise the money privately or to rely on the Committee to choose an architect. The final decision had to be made within three weeks and they needed to find £1,200. By the end of a fortnight, half that sum was collected and the two conspirators decided to guarantee the remainder. With some reluctance, the Committee accepted the proposal. Once again Morris had reason to be satisfied with his fund-raising technique. Among the contributions to the cost of the building was a gift of £8,000 from Chivers, the jam firm whose factory was in the adjoining village.

The plans for Impington represented the only constructive work that Gropius was offered in this country. When he had completed the project (on which he collaborated with Maxwell Fry) he left for America, where he was appointed Professor of Architecture at Harvard. Morris was never able to renew his friendship, but there is evidence to suggest Gropius gained something tangible from his brief encounter with the initiator of village colleges. In 1961, when he received the Kaufman International Design Award, he asked what it would take 'to rise above the cloud of false values which is smothering us'. He answered himself : purposeful, intensive education.

Then he said : 'It seems to be unimaginable that human nature should not rebel against the conspiracy to replace "the tree of Life" with a sales spiral. I hope this generation will, by the power of education, produce men who eventually will blaze a trail out of the commercial jungle.'

Morris inspired the sentiment and shared the hope.

Impington Village College was completed in 1939. Educationists reacted cautiously to the finished work, but enlightened students of architecture offered unqualified praise. To some, the long graceful lines of the building were simply a welcome change from the heavy and pretentious constructions that were part of the university expansion. Others were impressed by the designer's talent to improve on the facilities normally available to students. One visitor concluded, 'Nothing in this plan is extravagant or luxurious : everything is natural, functional, and practical. ...'

Nikolaus Pevsner, writing in *The Buildings of England*, Cambridgeshire volume, describes the College as 'One of the best buildings of its date in England, if not the best. ... The pattern for much to come (including most progressive schools built after the Second World War), in so far as at Impington the practical and visual advantages of modern forms in a loose yet coherent, completely free-looking arrangement had first been demonstrated.'

And Sir Herbert Read, in *Education through Art*, asks '... is it possible, not merely to conceive, but to build and introduce into the existing educational system, schools which provide the essentials of an educative environment? The answer is yes; it has been done in at least one instance (Impington), and a model perhaps not perfect in every detail, but practical, functional and beautiful, does exist on English soil.'

For Henry Morris, Impington was more than a bright new centre for rural education. He looked upon it as a highly valuable personal possession that others must treat with the respect and admiration they would normally reserve for a unique work of art. His entire staff were accustomed to his frequent appeals for administrative perfection (on one occasion during a visit to Sawston he was outraged to discover that the fountain was not playing) but he made exceptional demands upon those he had honoured by granting them employment at Impington. Even the gardener was expected to devote uncommon energy to his work. When he was criticized for allowing a few autumn leaves to remain on the lawn for an hour or so after they had fallen, his plea that 'at this time of year the leaves are falling all the time, and I can't do anything about it' was summarily dismissed as a totally inadequate excuse.

Immediately after this encounter Morris insisted on driving with some of his colleagues to the Fellows' Garden at Clare College just to see how landscaping could be improved by proper care and attention. As he stood absorbing the cloistered atmosphere, his deputy, George Edwards, pointed out the abundance of fallen leaves. Morris came out of his daydream :

'What do you expect in autumn?' he snapped.

By 1939 the Cambridgeshire village colleges were an established and nationally recognized feature of British education. Their success both as schools and as institutes for adult instruction and recreation was proved by the consistently enthusiastic support of the local communities. On average, each college had a winter evening attendance of four hundred men and women, who studied subjects ranging from metalcraft to ballet. Yet the experiment was not repeated elsewhere – at least, for the time being. Part of the problem was the lack of funds. It cost nothing for the Board of Education to urge local authorities to design senior schools with the community idea in mind, but the councils were also reminded (this time by voters and pressure groups) of the need to economize on rates and there was no hope that another Henry Morris would miraculously guide them to lush reserves of private capital.

For his own part, Morris was dissatisfied with the prospect of piecemeal educational reforms, undertaken by local authorities if and when surplus capital was allocated to the construction of new schools. The process of rethinking education priorities was certain to be frustratingly slow and laborious unless there was a sense of national purpose to stimulate the movement. In the early years of the Second World War he designed and promoted a blueprint of a school system that he hoped would be inaugurated at Government level once peace terms were settled. He outlined his plans in a memorandum addressed to the Association of Directors and Secretaries for Education and urged his colleagues to base their reasoning on the proposition that 'the final object of all future community planning, whether urban or rural, is cultural'. He elaborated his notion of cultural purposes by including under that heading '. . . health education from nursery stage to eighteen, adult education, social and physical recreation in community centres, and the consumption and practice of all the arts by the adult community'. It followed that his long-term aim was to transform every local community into an educational society and as a first step '. . . the development of an ubiquitous and fully articulated system of adult education should be regarded as the most important part of reconstruction after the war.' Morris calculated that a widespread system of adult education would '. . .enable us at long last to face up to the main fallacy of post-primary education . . . that to too great an extent it endeavours to educate the boy or girl at puberty or adolescence in terms of adult maturity.'

He may have underestimated the intellectual ability of young teenagers but he was surely right to chastise those schools (not in Cambridgeshire) where *King Lear* and *Paradise Lost* were typical samples of the cultural diet administered to thirteen-year-old pupils. For the sake of those teachers who believed that such mental exertions were academically beneficial (and the attitude still exists today) Morris referred to the 1937 edition of the *Handbook of Suggestions for Teachers*, where the theory of pumping children with extensive but superficial knowledge was carried to its ludicrous conclusion. The authors of the history section maintained that by the time a pupil left elementary school at the age of fourteen he should:

> ... have some idea of the stage in world history at which British history begins; of the people that were merged in the English nation; of the main social and economic changes through which the country has passed in the last thousand years; of the development of the national system of government; of the growth of the Empire; and of the present position of the British Commonwealth of Nations in the world. Above all, he should have begun to realize also that this story has some bearing on everyday life, and that the England of today and the British Commonwealth of Nations are the result of changes that can be traced through centuries.

When the student had absorbed this information, there were the intricacies of world history to consider, and finally it was suggested that any remaining time might be used to study the ancient civilizations of Palestine, Greece and Rome. The architects of this comprehensive syllabus concluded with an ironic note of indulgence: 'This is the ideal, but it is recognized that to attain it fully may be beyond the reach of many schools.'

Morris added: 'The assumption that the child between eleven and fourteen, or indeed fifteen, is intellectually, aesthetically and mentally a grown-up person appears in many other sections of the handbook, including those on English, Geography, Science, and the Arts. ... The same assumption pervades whole sections of other reports of the Board of Education and the Consultative Committee, for instance ... the Hadow Report, the more recent Spens Report, and various specialist reports on Secondary School curricula. '

Aside from his appeal for organized adult education, Morris

recommended that the school leaving age should be raised to sixteen ('To think in terms of raising the school leaving age to fifteen only introduces a factor of confusion into all our thoughts and planning about buildings, the curriculum, and staffing') and proposed the setting-up of day continuation schools for the age period sixteen to eighteen. More tentatively he suggested that '... we should ... discuss whether it is desirable or not to introduce an element of compulsion for some form of intellectual and physical training between the ages of eighteen and twenty-one.'

While he was prepared to extend the principle of compulsion in the state system of education, he was reluctant to call in the assistance of the legislators to combat what he described as the '... intellectual and spiritual and moral damage' caused by the public schools. He seemed to imagine that it was impossible to '... prevent the continuance of schools based on the plutocratic principle'. But '... we can at least explore their true nature in the hope that every gentle-man and gentle-woman whatever their economic class will refuse their support and reinforce the demand for a common system of education so that the realm of values may also be the realm of social unity.'

It was a pious hope; but if Morris was occasionally over-optimistic in his plans for educational reform at least he was able to see clearly the defects and limitations of the system as it existed then, and, with minor qualifications, still exists today. In one of the most perceptive chapters in his report he protested that the control of education '... both locally and centrally is administrative and not cultural'. He continued :

Neither administrators nor administration (in which I include inspection) can create and inform true education; they can ensure formal efficiency (an important commodity, but achieved by ants and bees), but they cannot create and sustain authentic sanctions. ... The proper architects of education are philosophers, artists, scientists, prophets and scholars, operating in freedom.

The teachers, many after inadequate education and training, are sent to the schools and there they remain, many forgotten for years, some for a lifetime. Some, it is true, but too few, go to refresher courses once, twice or thrice in their careers. Some authorities have weekly courses on Saturday mornings. We have neglected to devise for the teachers a system for their cultural sustenance and continued training in the art of teaching throughout the whole of their working careers. From this point of view the system of inspection is of little or no value. The system of organizers for various subjects as it at present exists is often too casual and superficial.

It is a state of affairs for which we have got to find a remedy. For myself, I think that we have to examine the possibility of linking up all the schools in an area to the regional University and its Education Department. We could place the educational welfare of schools and the cultural and technical guidance of the teachers in the regional care of the Universities of England and Wales, leaving the administration and administrative control in the hands of Local and Central Authorities.

There would thus be two influences guiding the education system – on the one hand the administrative control of the Local Education Authority and on the other the qualitative, intellectual and spiritual inspiration of the Universities effectively sustaining the cultural life of the teachers and reinforcing their capacity in the art of teaching. Under some such arrangement there would be constant traffic between the schools and the University and its departments. Teacher training would not end at twenty-one or twenty-two; it would be regarded as a permanent process going on throughout the teacher's career.

The final section of the report consisted of sundry recommendations that were intimately associated with his work in Cambridgeshire. He attacked the art schools for their failure to influence commercial design and demanded a concerted effort to establish 'visual awareness' as a proper function of education. He appealed for a higher standard in the architectural features of school buildings and deplored the narrow imagination of the 'official' architects. Free midday meals for all children were advocated, not so much on humanitarian grounds (poor families were, in any case, entitled to assistance) but more in the hope that the common meal would become an essential part of the life and training of the school. He forecast that, in the long run, the development of a universal system of post-primary education would obviate the need for a special-place examination at the age of eleven and, in anticipation of a society in which there was 'equality of consideration', he advocated that 'community education' should replace the dry phrase 'state education'.

A heavily watered-down version of his ideas was incorporated in the Orange Book which the Association of Directors and Secretaries of Education submitted to the Minister. Morris was naturally disappointed, but he might have accepted the collective report with better grace if it had been written in a style that the layman could appreciate. Instead, the weight of administrative jargon was too great for such a frail craft and it sank without trace. Morris exhausted his fury on those members of his staff who dared to repeat the error of writing letters and minutes in the stilted language of 'administratese'.

His speeches and correspondence of the war period show that Morris no longer recognized any real distinction between the educational and cultural problems of rural areas and of towns. His appeal for a universal system of adult education was linked with a proposal to design urban schools on the lines of community centres, so that they could be used to maximum advantage at all times during the day and throughout the year. The idea was attractive to the Government's educational advisers, who were attempting, under the leadership of R. A. Butler, the new President of the Board of Education, to formulate a post-war plan for raising the national standard of literacy without creating impossible burdens for the Exchequer. In March 1943, a representative of the Deputy Prime Minister made a tour of the village colleges and prepared a report for Clement Attlee which later found its way to Chuter Ede, Butler's Parliamentary Secretary. While admitting that '... the atmosphere of vitality, happiness, culture and sunlight came as a great stimulus to me personally when I remember the elementary schools that I attended as a small boy ...', the writer offered two criticisms of the educational system in Cambridgeshire. First :

The scale of the work in the stiffer and more formal kind of adult education is not remarkable. Even at Impington the classes are no larger than can be found in any place of the same size where there is a well-organized branch of the W.E.A., despite the fact that the facilities for the work are far better. This relative failure is wholly due, I am sure, to the absence of a capable and experienced Tutor Organizer on the staff of the College and Mr Morris is fully aware of this point and plans are in hand to appoint such people in future, and indeed, one or two have just been appointed.

When Morris studied the report he added a postcript to say that tutor organizers had recently been appointed to all the colleges. Secondly :

I found that the Wardens were a little indifferent and short-sighted in their attitude to and use of the cinema. At Impington the average attendance for the class in Current Affairs was twelve (maintained with some difficulty) while 250 to 300 people would pay 3d. or 6d. to come to see a film. Yet the Warden did not appear to appreciate the fundamental significance of these figures. His attitude was partly due to the Puritanism still lingering among the local population. Nevertheless, he did plainly feel that the film was inferior as a form of 'educational' activity and he said that he was not himself interested in the cinema or in the habit of seeing films. This I felt to be a pity.

The report claimed that the existence of the colleges

raised urgent problems for the future development of our educational and recreational policy. The Board of Education are going to make part-time attendance at Day Continuation Schools compulsory under the new Act and they have accepted the responsibility for pressing forward the construction of a large number of Community Centres. Presumably the execution of these two policies will require the construction of a number of new buildings. I wonder if the appropriate steps have been taken to bring these two developments into one consistent plan ? There is plainly much to be said for the provision of all these facilities in one building on the model of the Village College.

Buildings are, however, less than half the story. Unsuitable administrators can render useless the most extravagant physical equipment. The best type of man or woman can work miracles in the dreariest surroundings. There is every reason for giving the workman the best tools, but only the best workman can use them.

Everything depends upon the recruitment of good Wardens for the Community Centres. What sort of people ought they to be and what kind of training can be provided for them? The answer to this question depends in part upon the plan for the buildings. If the Community Centre is normally to contain a Senior School, the Warden must be capable of acting as, or supervising sympathetically, the Headmaster of such a school. It is, however, difficult to believe that the Headmasters of most elementary schools are suitable people to deal with adolescents, much less to solve the intricate and obstinate problems of adult education. On the other hand, it would seem a thousand pities not to bring these various branches of education into one beautiful and well-equipped building.

The Government's proposals for revitalizing the schools and universities were set out in a White Paper submitted to Parliament in July 1943. On a professional and personal level, Henry Morris had reason to be encouraged by the scope of the recommendations. It was intended that the administrative authorities should be given statutory responsibility for an educational process that extended from nursery schools to adult education and embraced recreational facilities, youth services and residential courses. Morris disputed the need to divide education into grammar, secondary and technical streams for children over the age of eleven, but the intention to raise the school leaving age to sixteen and to examine the means by which the public schools could be associated with the national system received his unqualified approval.

Also encouraging to Morris were the clauses in the White Paper announcing that fees in state secondary schools were to be abolished and the provision of milk and meals extended. Most important of all was the provision for compulsory part-time education up to the age of eighteen for children who left school at the minimum age. R. A. Butler and his colleagues avoided a definite commitment to the village-college philosophy (they were possibly deterred by the scarcity of head teachers who possessed the essential range of academic and administrative talent) and instead recommended the setting-up of county colleges where a variety of cultural, civic and technical subjects could be provided. Morris and his work in Cambridgeshire received favourable mention in the House of Commons debate on the White Paper and Chuter Ede, who wound up for the Government, referred to the Impington experiment as 'one that need not be slavishly followed elsewhere, but ... an idea which can be adapted to the requirement of the different areas.'

The Butler Act became law on 3 August 1944 but the failure, even now, to implement all the provisions of the Bill emphasizes the difference between Morris, who acted on his principles, and most of his administrative contemporaries who were happy enough to leave the initiative to the Government and to accept the dictum that major reforms were impracticable at a local level. In Cambridge, the education plan approved by the Council in 1930 was brought up to date and provision was made for the building of seven more village colleges. The blueprint was subsequently revised to take account of changes in national economic policy and unforeseen administrative problems, but in broad terms the education structure envisaged by Morris was completed in July 1966 when the last village college was opened at Burwell. It was here, forty-three years earlier, that he had established the first senior school in the county.

The frustrations of leading a pressure group for a new philosophy of education left Morris without the reserves of patience necessary to contend with the inevitable wartime restrictions. Not least of his worries was the shortage of qualified staff and he regularly complained that greater efforts should have been made to secure military exemption for his professional sympathizers. In particular, he missed George Hawes, an extrovert Yorkshireman who possessed the courage, if not always the energy, to talk with Morris on equal terms. 'The Office is going to pot,' Morris told the Chief Clerk on one occasion, 'and all because of your pusillanimity, if I may say so, in failing to reserve Hawes. *You must get him back.*' In fact, no one could have prevented Hawes from volunteering at the earliest opportunity. He had reached the point where any change from the turbulent Morris – even the front line – was as good as a rest.

The administrative routine during the war years was enlivened by the extravagant demands the Chief Education Officer made upon his staff and the emotionally exhausting reprimands that ensued when they failed to live up to his high expectations. His secretary recalls :

'It was as if one dwelt on Olympus, with Zeus ever-present hurling thunderbolts. His "Do you agree?" at the close of a tirade was thunderous in intensity, if not in actual volume. Sometimes the thunder was muted, but not lessened in effectiveness thereby. He might appear at the door, speak one's name in almost a drawl, or simply beckon one to follow. ... Then he would lead the way along the corridor with his quick light step which was somehow indicative of the verbal rapier-thrusts of the interview that followed. This interview was invariably a masterly, a diabolically masterly, probing and pursuing through questioning, until each cravenly concealed fault or inadequacy was brought into the daylight. Then – "God Almighty!" he would thunder, casting his eyes to Heaven for strength to bear with such stupidity, such crassness, such unparalleled ineptness. And in tones of withering scorn, "You amateurs!"'

The 'amateurs' occasionally dreamed of the day of release and when, in late 1946, it was announced that Morris had been appointed Cultural Adviser to the Minister of Town and Country Planning, many of his staff shared a secret hope that his latest responsibilities would provide a welcome distraction from their supposed deficiencies. The local paper heralded the news of the Chief Education Officer's advancement with the startling headline 'Mr Silkin wants Mr Morris' and a member of the County Hall team whose dignity Morris had successfully punctured was heard to remark, 'Mr Silkin can have Mr Morris.'

His brief from the Ministry of Town and Country Planning was to advise on the cultural aspects of construction and development of the new towns that were part of the Government building programme. For a job of this nature he had few competitors. His village colleges were an original and important

173

experiment in community living, but of equal significance were his critical interest in architecture and his proposals for counteracting the baser influences of urban growth and industrialization.

Between 1945 and 1946 Morris concentrated much of his time on the broad problems of town planning. He railed against those communities where 'ugliness is accepted as normal, beauty regarded as a luxury or even eccentric' and in a letter to a friend he argued that:

'... the town and countryside must be planned so that they will provide a way of life (the new democratic way of life). The alternative is more barbarism and militarism (and Fascism). I think that we might lead the world here. The reactionaries say that democracy cannot evolve a culture and will not know how to use the artists. We have to disprove this.'

He was increasingly aware of the cultural limitations of schools and colleges (even village colleges) and his definition of education was broadened to include the creative work in theatres, concert halls, community and recreation centres. Above all, he emphasized 'the aesthetic character of building and landscape as a cultural instrument'.

The relatively tolerant atmosphere in the education offices satisfied his staff that Morris was grateful to the Ministry for the opportunity to put his ideas into practice. But before he could get down to the business of translating ideals into practicabilities he had to fulfil an obligation to the Colonial Office, who invited him to spend two months in West Africa and make recommendations on the structure of further education in these developing countries. He left England just before Christmas 1946 and immediately on his arrival in Africa entered on a long round of meetings and receptions. His grand tour was a successful exercise in public relations but in terms of educational advancement the results were meagre. This was not entirely the fault of Morris, whose scope for investigation was tightly restricted, but his report was overweighted with a long-winded appeal for an Institute of Architecture and he made few concessions to the unique characteristics of African culture. In any case, there was a delay of almost a year before he found time to submit his recommendations and though he hoped to reveal to the Colonial Office 'possibilities more than they had dreamed of,' he had no reason to be surprised when he received nothing more than a perfunctory acknowledgement.

The disappointment was quickly forgotten in the rush to complete the development plans for education in Cambridge-shire and to produce a comprehensive memorandum for sub-mission to the corporations of each of the new towns. Represen-tatives from Harlow, Crawley, Welwyn Garden City, Hatfield, Stevenage, Hemel Hempstead, Aycliffe and Bracknell were escorted on conducted tours of the village colleges and intro-duced to the basic principles of the Morris philosophy. In particular, they were invited to take account of the theory that buildings designed for social and educational activities should form a recognizable group so that the units could inter-link their contributions and foster the concept of a united and active community.

Working on the assumption that a new town would support a population of about 60,000 Morris argued that, in addition to a centre grouping, there should be three campuses 'each placed at a selected point between the centre and the periphery of the town and each serving approximately a third of the population'. But of first importance was the construction of the nerve centre of the community :

The College of Further Education ought to be an important and significant part of the central square or squares, where the adminis-trative and the cultural should, so to speak, be blended. Thus there should be a close association between the College of Further Educa-tion, and the art gallery, the concert hall and the town's main library, all three of which will be conceived on livelier and more imaginative lines than in the past. These buildings should have some relation to the town's administrative centre, so that in the result education will not be separated from the active appreciation and practice of the Arts and all of them will not be entirely divorced from civic administration. One example of what might be aimed at is to be found in St Mark's Square at Venice with the Doge's Palace, the Cathedral, the Courts of Justice, the Library, Municipal Offices, etc., surrounding perhaps the most potent and moving space in Europe. The theatre has also to be remembered. There is no need to be dogmatic about the actual form of the location of these public buildings in addition to the law court and other administrative buildings. It is possible for them to be placed in very significant relationship even if they are placed in two communicating squares or spaces. The important thing that has been said is to associate education with ordinary life and both with the practice of the Arts and with civic administration.

Morris intended that the three subsidiary groupings should cater for secondary schools, county colleges, further education and community centres, branch libraries and, possibly, health centres. He claimed that these campuses, which he labelled A, B and C, would be easily accessible to the users and would lend 'great significance, both cultural and architectural, to the body of the town'. He went on :

For a town of 60,000 there might be three *selective* secondary schools (one three-form entry grammar school for some 630 boys, one three-form entry grammar school for some 630 girls, and one three-form entry technical high school for some 630 boys *and* girls). These schools would not be placed in isolation in various points near the centre of the town. The boys' grammar school would be on A campus, the girls' grammar school would be on B campus and the technical high school would be on C campus.

At *each* campus, there would be placed two modern schools, one for boys and one for girls, each to serve approximately a third of the town area.

The location and the curriculum of the County College are problems about which no clear lead has been given by the Ministry of Education and in the country generally there is difference of opinion. The truth is that there is more than one answer to both problems and that there is room for experiment. The number of boys and girls of fifteen to eighteen in a town of 60,000 who will attend the County College on one day a week will be about 2,000 (400 pupils a day).

Apart from day work, the County College is intended to provide club life for young people in the evenings and at weekends. Clearly, there are serious objections to providing for the whole group of

176

2,000 in one centre, either in isolation (since the County College ought to be in a context that looks towards maturity) or on the same site as the College of Further Education. An evening concourse of 500 to 1,000 young people would be a mob rather than a club; and the clubs should be an intimate and human unit in which the young man or woman can feel that they really matter. It is therefore suggested that the County College should be divided into three units, one to be placed on each of the three campuses where its association with the community centre would provide a context looking towards maturity. Each unit would provide for between six and seven hundred young people. Here would be provided a training on one day a week for each boy and girl in continued education and practical activities. ... There would be some vocational training both in the day time and in the evening, but specific vocational education of a systematic and advanced character would be provided at the College of Further Education to which selected boys and girls from trades and callings (e.g. printing, building, dress-design) could be sent. While accommodation, including club rooms, would be specially set apart for the County College group at each campus, there would be certain facilities which could be shared in common (e.g. gymnasia, playing fields, tennis, fives and squash courts, etc.).

The Community Centre would have some buildings of its own (e.g. Branch Library, adult lecture room, common rooms, games rooms and a committee room are essential), but as it would be placed near the secondary school many of the rooms belonging to the latter, e.g. workshops, domestic science rooms, laboratories, etc., would be available for use by adults in the evenings. The community centre would provide for young people and adults of all ages a balanced programme of classes and courses at a less systematic level than at the town's College of Further Education. There would be provision for crafts and hobbies, for instrumental music and singing, and for drama.

At the time when Morris was setting out his proposals, there were no Ministry regulations governing the land allocation to schools with more than 450 pupils. He took advantage of this omission by urging the development corporations of the new towns to plan generously in the expectation that other local authorities would follow their example. But his interpretation of the phrase 'minimum requirements' was judged to be unrealistic by the central administrators who, three years later, published their own calculations. In the Morris plan, a secondary modern catering for at least 600 pupils required a site not smaller than twenty-five and a half acres (a four-acre garden was included in the estimate). The Ministry argued that a school of this size needed no more than thirteen and a half acres and in 1954 the allocation dropped to ten acres, apparently to take account of new methods of economizing on land.

Morris had better luck with his forecast of the changes in the organization of secondary education. His plans anticipated the introduction of comprehensive schools (but not, interestingly enough, co-educational schools) on a national scale and he suggested the means by which the amalgamation of the grammar and secondary modern systems could be implemented painlessly and inexpensively:

> The course recommended ... is to give the modern schools and the grammar schools and the technical high school the same standard of buildings and amenities and to put them in association on the same campus. Thus the grammar school will not be isolated, and the three types of secondary school will be placed in an identical physical context. They would have many contacts as, for example, in meeting each other on the football field, in debate and perhaps in choruses, opera, drama and orchestra. The three schools might have the same coat of arms with a slight deviation for the modern school, the grammar school and the technical high school. It is suggested that serious consideration should be given to the provision of a fine chapel at each campus, to be used jointly by all the secondary schools.

The benefits of campus education were not widely recognized until the late 1950s, when the plan was adopted by the Leicestershire authority. The experiment prompted the attention of many admirers but few imitators.

Despite the effort that Morris put into his part-time job as cultural adviser, the results were disappointing. Occasionally, by sheer pressure of energy and self-confidence, he was able to force through decisions that encouraged him to think that he could achieve a breakthrough. When the College of Further

Education was constructed at Welwyn Garden City, he persuaded the urban district council to contribute sufficient money to incorporate a fine concert hall. He failed in his ambition to raise sufficient funds to purchase Henry Moore's sculpture 'Family Group' and was intensely jealous of John Newsom – then Chief Education Officer of Hertfordshire – who acquired it for one of his secondary modern schools. But as something of a compensation he was instrumental in setting up the Digswell Arts Trust, which sponsored an experimental artists' community based on a converted Regency house. 'We have to come to terms with leisure and affluence,' wrote Morris, 'but we shall not do so unless on the lines of pursuing beauty and order.' The Digswell project was his unique contribution to the creative arts and he expected his little band of prodigies to be the focal point of a great adventure in education.

But, like so many of his ideas, the scheme was not allowed the chance of wider application and eventually Morris had to admit that a few isolated successes did not add up to a cultural revolution. Even on his home territory, in Cambridgeshire, progress was slow and sporadic. New village colleges were planned but he failed in his ambition to rebuild the technical college which he had hoped would lead the way in developing an education that combined practical skills with an appreciation of the humanities.

Morris was near the end of his career. He divided his energies between the administration of Cambridgeshire and the cultural development of the new towns, and the work was simply too much for a man who was running short of patience and enthusiasm. 'It would mean a fight,' he said, referring on one occasion to a controversial proposal. 'I'm too old to fight.' His health was another liability. In December 1947, in his capacity as a member of the Education Advisory Committee for the Royal Air Force, he spent a weekend at a bleakly situated air base. The result was his first attack of pneumonia, an illness which he never entirely defeated.

He retired as Chief Education Officer for Cambridgeshire in

1954. Four years later he moved to a flat in Welwyn Garden City so that he could be close to his dream project, the Digswell Arts Trust Centre. He was praised and flattered by sympathizers who noted that at last the village college idea was catching on (Peterborough, Monmouthshire and Derbyshire introduced schemes modelled on the Cambridgeshire plan), but from the friends who watched him in physical and mental decline he elicited the overriding sentiment of pity. In late 1959 he suffered another attack of pneumonia which, complicated by other illnesses, led to a hardening of the arteries and a degeneration of brain capacity. In hospital, his natural eccentricities were interpreted as symptoms of advanced abnormality and he spent a period in an institution for the mentally sick until Jack Pritchard and his wife (a psychiatrist) succeeded in having him transferred to a nursing home in Cambridge.

Occasionally, he managed to rediscover his enthusiasm for living and he brightened when he was in the company of young people:

'They will be my ambassadors for the future,' he told Jack Pritchard when he was introduced to his friend's grandchildren, but shortly afterwards he was lost again in a mood of despondency. His last public appearance was at the opening of Comberton Village College in 1960. He made a depressing speech which he repeated three times before the chairman caught him by the sleeve and persuaded him to sit down. George Edwards, his successor as Chief Education Officer, described it as 'a moving and tragic experience'.

In common with most successful men, Henry Morris left many ambitions unfulfilled. One of his greatest hopes was to be made a peer or at the very least to be elevated to a Companion of Honour – not, perhaps, an idealistic aspiration, but he was honest enough to admit the need for an indication that his work had not passed unnoticed. A group of his friends petitioned R. A. Butler who suggested to the Minister of Education that Morris should be considered for 'a high honour'. At the same time he warned: 'there are so many deserving candidates that I cannot give any assurance about the outcome.'

The award was never made and when Morris died in late 1961, he was still a mere C.B.E. His rivals and critics in education – academics, philosophers and grand administrators among them – who thought, but seldom acted, in terms of national change possibly regarded this as a just penalty for a man whose reputation rested more on small-scale successes than large-scale illusions.

Bibliography

The following list of books, pamphlets and papers is by no means a complete record of those consulted in the writing of this book, but forms a guide to the literature for those who would like to pursue further the stories it contains.

The Malting House School: 1924–9

ISAACS, NATHAN, *Early Scientific Trends in Children*, National Froebel Foundation, 1928.
> A pamphlet taking further the discussion begun in the 'Why' questions appendix (see Isaacs, Susan, below). It draws heavily on experience gained at Malting House.

ISAACS SUSAN, *The Nursery Years*, Routledge & Kegan Paul, 1929.
> A parental guide, still valid today, published shortly after the break with Pyke at Cambridge.

Intellectual Growth in Young Children, with an Appendix on children's 'Why' questions by Nathan Isaacs, Routledge & Kegan Paul, 1930.

Social Development in Young Children, Routledge & Kegan Paul, 1933.
> These two books are the direct outcome of the Malting House studies and form the high-water mark in the literature of child development in Britain. The material on which they were based was compiled by the secretarial staff mentioned in the text.

Bibliography

> *The Psychological Aspects of Child Development*, University of London Institute of Education and Evans Bros., sixth printing, 1965.
>
> This booklet first appeared as Section 11 of the 1935 volume of *The Year Book of Education*. It embodies much that Susan Isaacs learnt at Malting House on the psychology of infancy and early childhood.

LAMPE, DAVID, *Pyke: The Unknown Genius*, Evans Bros., 1959.

> A book dealing with the early life of Geoffrey Pyke, but more particularly with the latter period during the Second World War.

'Scientific Interests of a Boy in the Preschool Years', by two parents, in *The Forum of Education*, vol. VI, no. 1, February 1928.

The Burston Rebellion: 1914

Burston Parish Council minutes, 1913–16.

Burston School Managers' Minute Book, 1911–19.

'CASEY', 'The Burston Strike School', pamphlet published by the *Labour Leader*, 1916.

EDWARDS, GEORGE, *From Crow Scaring to Westminster*, Labour Publishing Co., 1922.

GROVES, REG, *Sharpen the Sickle: The History of the Farm Workers Union*, Porcupine Press, 1949.

HIGDON, THOMAS, *The Mock Memorial Tablet.*
The Persecution of a Poor Man by a Parson.

> Two pamphlets, privately circulated, dealing with the Henry Garnham case.

Prussianism in Norfolk.

> A private pamphlet dealing with the Burston School strike.

The Burston Rebellion, National Labour Press, 1920.

> Higdon's own detailed account of the strike.

National Union of Agricultural Workers, Records 1913–20.

National Union of Teachers, Records 1913–20.

Norfolk County Council, minutes of Education Committee 1913–20.

Report on Burston School Strike, 5 January 1917.

Schoolteacher, The, November 1913–July 1915.
For reports on Dowlais School strike.

WILBY, EMILY, *Our School Strike.*
Pamphlet published by the Burston School Strike Committee.

Art and Craft

BLACKIE, JOHN, *Inside the Primary School,* Department of Education and Science, H.M.S.O., 1967.

Primary Education, H.M.S.O., 1959.

RICHARDSON, MARION, *Art and the Child,* University of London Press, 1948.

TANNER, ROBIN, *Children's Work in Block-Printing,* Dryad Press, Leicester, 1936.
Lettering for Children, Dryad Press, Leicester, sixth edn, 1962.

The Forest School: 1929–38

WESTLAKE, AUBREY, The Woodcraft Way Series.
This series, which formed the written core of the philosophy of the Order of Woodcraft Chivalry, is largely out of print, but copies can still be obtained through British Monomark or the agencies of the Forest School Camps. The series consisted of the following titles :
1. *Woodcraft,* by Ernest Thompson Seton
2. *The Theory of Woodcraft Chivalry*
3. *Woodcraft Chivalry*
4. *Primitive Occupations as a Factor in Education*
5. *The Adventurer's Handbook*
6. *How to Run Woodcraft Chivalry: Deeds, Trials and Adventures,* by Ernest Westlake
7. *The Forest School and Other Papers: The Principles of Education of the O.W.G.,* by Ernest Westlake

Bibliography

   8. *Hints for Running Groups*, by Grey Beaver (typescript)
   9. *The Place of Dionysos*, by Ernest Westlake
 11. *The Council System: Part 1 – The Lodge*, by Golden Eagle
 14. *The Biological Principles of Education*, by Jennings H. D. White

Henry Morris: 1889–1961

BAKER, W. P., *The English Village*, O.U.P., 1953.

Cambridgeshire and Isle of Ely Education Committee, Minutes 1922–

HADOW, SIR W. H., *Report of the Consultative Committee of the Board of Education of the Adolescent*, Board of Education, 1926.

MORRIS, HENRY, *The Village College*, private pamphlet, 1924.
  Memorandum to the Association of Directors and Secretaries of Education, 1942.

PEVSNER, NIKOLAUS, *The Buildings of England: Cambridgeshire*, Penguin Books, 1953.

READ, SIR HERBERT, *Education through Art*, Faber & Faber, 1943.

TAWNEY, R. H., *Secondary Education for All*, Labour Party, 1924.

Index

187

Index

188

Index